THROUGH MIGHTY SEAS

FRONTISPIECE

The Author

THROUGH MIGHTY SEAS

SEAS

The Romance of a Little Wind-jammer

by

Lt. Col. HENRY HUGHES

Second Edition

19 75

T. STEPHENSON & SONS LTD.
PRESCOT, MERSEYSIDE

By the same author
IMMORTAL SAILS

Second edition published 1975

ISBN 0 901314 17 X

Printed by
T. STEPHENSON & SONS LTD., PRESCOT, MERSEYSIDE

THE SECOND EDITION

This book is republished in memory of my dear father in the year of the one hundredth anniversary of his birth in Portmadoc.

I feel that with the tremendous enthusiasm in sailing today there are many who may read these pages with great interest.

CAPTAIN JAMES HENRY A. HUGHES, E.R.D.,
Bryn y Ddwyryd,
Tan y Bwlch,
Blaenau Ffestiniog,
Gwynedd.

FOREWORD

This tale of the sea is culled from the diaries of a boy who, in the early 'nineties, for reasons of health, was sent to sea in a wind-jammer and did three voyages in the barque *Pride of Wales*, sailing out of Portmadoc to the South Americas and the West Indies.

Sail was dying even in those far-off days, and the *Pride of Wales*, though the largest vessel ever built by Simon Jones, was also one of the last of her kind to be fitted out at this old Welsh yard.

Reefing topsails in a freshening gale, rolling in a flat calm in the doldrums, scarcity of fresh water, the beauties of Rio de Janeiro and flying fish, and the almost miraculous cure of a sick man, are described each in their turn, and the book ends with the loss of this tall ship in a later voyage.

Anyone who can write with first-hand knowledge of life in a sailing ship forty or fifty years ago must surely find matters of interest to recount, and a retentive memory backed up by diaries here gives a glimpse of peoples and places in the days when life was more leisurely than is now the case.

J. A. EDGELL,
Vice-Admiral.

PORTMADOC

I hope I may claim the reader's indulgence while I briefly describe this little-known place, hidden in the rocky mountains of North Wales. I intend to deal with it purely as a port and shipbuilding centre, and hope in so doing not to incur the historian's displeasure.

It came into being, prospered, and receded into oblivion. In the number of years allotted to the life of man, there were a few who lived there who saw it pass through these three stages: necessity prompted its creators to fill these two roles. Thirteen miles away, climbing through enchanting scenery known as the Vale of Maentwrog, stands the town of Ffestiniog. It flourished as a slate quarrying centre. The artistic colouring and the durability of the stone soon brought fame to these obscure parts. Modern Europe and indeed other more distant continents clamoured for the Ffestiniog slates. They seemed to be the very things to crown their important architectural efforts. During the 1830s and '40s half-hearted attempts were indulged in to deal with the situation. Slates were carried by road in horse-drawn carts to a primitive quay built at the western end of the Maentwrog Vale—close to Penrhyndeudraeth. Here they were loaded into lighters, and when the tidal waters of Tremadoc Bay flushed along the banks of the Dwyryd, the barges floated and were rowed by the "Glaslyn Boatmen" to yet another home-made quay at Portmadoc, from where ships carried them to all parts of the world. The old quay at Penrhyn, with its rusty sling chains and ring bolts, can still be recognised today.

It was soon realised that this was not good enough, so the local people started to make a port and build ships. Much mud was scooped from the bed of the river Glaslyn to form a pretty harbour for accommodating incoming ships, rock was torn and blasted from the rugged sides of the hills to make wharves and quays, shipbuilding yards, repairing beaches, grids and the like seemed to drop from the clouds. Locomotives whistled round the corners (Festiniog Narrow-Gauge Railway), the put-put-put of steam tug boats was soon heard up and down the river, sailors and pilots, carpenters and riggers filled the foreshore, ship's chandlers and ship brokers offices opened their doors. Shipbuilding was taken on in earnest, the resounding din of the caulking mallet mingled pleasantly with the wail of the gull and the screech of the noisy crows. Portmadoc had taken shape and was on the map.

In 1890 it boasted of being the port of registry of nearly 300 sailing ships. The peak years of its prosperity ranged between 1870 and 1895. By 1900 is was virtually over. Green grass carpeted the quays and the old mud returned to the water-ways. Foreign competitors, steamers, railway competition and low freights took their inevitable toll. In spite of this short-lived success, it lasted long enough to make Portmadoc famous for all time. The little ships built there roamed the seven seas.

Known as the "Western Ocean Yachts", they added a lustrous page to the annals of British shipping in the great days of sail. Their beauty of design, grace of line, smoothness of rig and turn of speed made them the envy of maritime nations.

The shipbuilding enterprise can be divided into two epochs: one which finished about 1875 and evolved two types of vessels—a stout schooner to cater for coastal trade and the confined waters of northern Europe, larger ships of square rig destined to tackle

the deepest waters of the oceans, many brigs and bar-
quentines and two or three barques.

The gem of the fleet was undoubtedly the *Pride of
Wales*. Then came a hiatus and an experimental ship
(called the *C. E. Spooner*) was built with the idea of
embodying the former two types. She was a three-
masted schooner with double top sails and top gallant
yard across. Besides being a good looker, she was
strong and speedy. She was followed by an improved
large two-masted schooner called the *Richard Greaves*,
yet another experiment. She was greatly admired and
looked full of promise. Built entirely of Welsh oak and
her hull copper covered, she was recommended for any
part of the world, but the *C. E. Spooner* type seemed the
better, and in 1890 an extensive programme of building
on these lines was adopted and carried through. A
cargo fleet was built in a very short time. They were
beautiful ships and a crowning success, so much so
that it was indeed difficult to make a choice between
them. The sailing record of each was carefully watched.
One little ship kept herself prominently in the limelight.
But old sailors are tough judges; they would not be
rushed into premature conclusions. The wee *Blodwen*,
however, hammered at their conscience. Record after
record she proudly carried to Portmadoc. She was
finally adjudged the queen. She feared nothing, great
or small. Even ocean records failed to frighten her.
She shaped up to them and beat them.

J. H. A. HUGHES.

CONTENTS

LIST OF ILLUSTRATIONS

AUTHOR'S NOTE

THE twentieth century has seen the passing from the face of the sea the gallant rear-guard of an era of sail that had lasted hundreds of years.

In our time much has been written about these aristocrats of the deep—the famous China tea clippers; the Nitrate carriers; the wool clippers, and the Australian grain ships. But the heroine of this book is one of those tiny ships, one of an enormous fleet that sailed the seas little noticed or known. Few of them carried more than five hundred tons. Their length rarely exceeded a hundred and forty feet, and their deck clearance of the sea (free board) could be gauged in inches. Yet there was no useful nook or accessible cranny on the earth's seaboard where they could not be found bobbing to their anchors, with the assurance of a warship having finished a passage of five or ten thousand miles across the great oceans.

They proudly and efficiently did their share in knitting together our great and far-flung Empire.

They plied regularly to our small and lonely islands and settlements dotted about the barren wastes of the seas. There they were especially useful, being easily handled in primitive harbours. Many of them were both speedy and elegant of design. The West Country, including Wales, specialised in their building; keen competition existed in the various small ports of Devon,

Cornwall, and Wales for the prettiest design combined with sea-worthiness and speed.

I spent my early days in these ships; and although as I have said they have now virtually passed from the face of the sea, some of these smaller craft actually kept on until the days of the Great War. During those nerve-racking and strenuous years, I went to sea again, and commanded one of His Majesty's patrol boats stationed off the bleak and inhospitable Cornish coast. The work was to deal with enemy submarines and protect shipping. Every member of the ship's company knew that I had seen service in sailing ships. On that account no occasion was lost in getting me involved if anything with a sail was seen. It is not difficult to imagine the excitement that ran throughout the ship when one day a signal was flashed to inform the patrols that a convoy of 117 French sailing vessels would shortly be passing through that area. It seemed almost incredible in the twentieth century that such an event would take place. It was a grand and noble sight. It made my veins bulge with magnetism. For a distance of thirty miles some six hundred sails embroidered a blue and sunny sky. Most of these sails belonged to a previous age. Patched with bits of canvas of many tints and manifold designs, they gave this war-scarred ocean a tranquil atmosphere and a touch of artistry. These tiny ships had been collected from every part of France and were doing valiant service. Their country was in dire need of coal, and they were sent to fetch it from South Wales.

My first thoughts were, what a harvest for energetic submarines; but the convoy, shepherded only by two French destroyers, passed unmolested through the active submarine zones. As a matter of fact it represented a fleet of no mean might, for each ship mounted that wonder gun the *soixante quinze*, at the breech of which stood a naval gunner complete with blue tam and red bobble. France was then in earnest.

．　　　．　　　．　　　．　　　．

I am confining this book to reminiscences during the last three completed voyages of a small Welsh barque called the *Pride of Wales.*

THROUGH MIGHTY SEAS

CHAPTER I

The Pride of Wales

LAYING THE KEEL

IN 1868 a certain David Morris set the small town of Portmadoc in North Wales all agog. He announced that he had decided to build a vessel half as big again as the largest ever built in the place, not only the largest in tonnage but the most ambitious in rig and detail. Her specifications were such that people of the place thought he had lost his reason.

David Morris, however, was not only an indomitable sailor, but the sea to him was a business. He had realised the needs of the future. He had an intuition that there was a place in the world for his dream ship. He visualised golden days by the coral strands of India. He gambled his all on the venture. I was able to gather much authentic information about those anxious and exciting days from a ship's carpenter, one John Hughes, who not only helped to build this pretty ship but also sailed in her.

It became known that the ship was to be called the *Pride of Wales*. This made David Morris's jealous contemporaries chuckle the more. In fact they were aghast at the man's audacity. Unruffled and determined, David Morris was found in constant and close consultations with Simon Jones, the designer who, for years, had yearned for an

FACE PAGE 14   JOHN BARTHOLOMEW AND SON LTD.

Map showing places traded by Portmadoc ships

Pride of Wales

opportunity to put his undoubted artistry into full effect. His chance had come.

"I know," said the owner to the designer, "that in my desire to call this ship the *Pride of Wales*, I have made it difficult for you and for me; but I feel I can look to you to overcome this difficulty."

Simon Jones made no mistake, and when the little vessel swung amidstream to her anchor on her launching day, each agreed to absolve the other from reproach and recriminations. They could face their critics with complete equanimity.

The keel was laid at Borth-y-Gest, near Portmadoc. If atmosphere induced inspiration it was to be found in this little place to a pleasing fullness. This pretty village lay between two bold headlands which jutted into a gurgling estuary. The jaunty dwellings of men of the sea followed the foreshore in a graceful curve and overlooked the bay. But one doubt existed. Was Borth-y-Gest sufficiently central and convenient as a ship-building centre?

The matter of conveying the huge oak lumbers, necessary for the work, along unmade and narrow roads, looked a problem not too easy of solution. But the stout hearts of eight heavy-draught horses turned the difficulty into a local entertainment.

Crowds used to gather at the foot of a steep hill known as Pen-y-Clogwyn for the sheer delight of seeing the great oak trees being galloped up this narrow ravine. The jangling chains of harness, the cracking of whips, the clatter of hoofs, and the encouraging shouts from the horsemen filled the air, while the villagers, hidden by the dust, revelled in the fun and pushed their utmost behind the fallen giants. Spars and sails, tackle and tanks, ropes and rigging, followed in an endless trek. Soon the wonder ship began to take shape. The gaunt hull towered above a host of pleasure craft and fishing boats which speckled the beach. Her elegant stern dipped over the tidal waters of the Atlantic. Her high bows peeped proudly over well-timbered meadowland undulating towards the shorn and rugged Moel-y-Gest which clouded the sky a mile away northwards. This characteristic piece of Welsh scenery added a touch of dignity to the recently-animated surroundings.

One day a farmer's cart came rumbling through the town and attracted attention. It carried a huge case rather like a sarcophagus. There was a rumour that it contained the figure-head of the new ship, and there were many stories circulating about it. A motley and curious cortège followed it to Borth-y-Gest, where they hoped to catch the first glimpse. In vain the procession, however. Only a few were to see the figure-head before it was really placed on the bows to herald the coming of the *Pride of Wales*.

When the people of Portmadoc did see the figure-head, they were very proud of it. A great deal of pains and craft had gone to the making of it. It represented a young girl of seventeen moving forward as it were with a sprightly gait. A wealth of waving hair covered her head, and it appeared to be ruffled and freshly blown by the winds of the sea. Her aquiline features were wreathed in a seraphic smile. A strand of coral adorned her neck, with pendant ear-rings in keeping —a symbol of the sea. Her dress was white and short, displaying shapely legs which, with their buckled shoes, rested on an elaborately-carved plinth tinged with gold and green. The right arm stretched over the sea, and in the hand was a red rose, an offering, to greet the sun or to humour the storm.

The launching day created a great deal of excitement, and was treated as a local holiday. Borthy-Gest turned gay. There were flags on every house, and the main street was festooned as though for a coronation. Every vantage point carried the slogan "*Good Luck, 'Pride of Wales'*." Shores and scaffolding were cleared away so that an uninterrupted view of the ship was available to all for the first time. Her lower masts and bowsprit only in position were festooned by gaudy code flags. A silken burgee thirty feet long, emblazoned with her name, flew from a staff on the main. The elaborate carving of sinuous reptiles in intertwined confusion, which completely covered her stern, was then unveiled for the first time.

All the sages were agreed that the ship was a joy to look upon, and that Simon Jones had reached the zenith of his career. Painted a rich bottle-green, girded with a gold strake, the *Pride of Wales* looked very much like a beautiful toy in a shop window.

Then the climax. . . .

The much - discussed figure - head was still shrouded in linen, but as soon as a tall young lady mounted the platform to perform the naming ceremony and to send the bottle of wine crashing against her bows, the shroud was torn away, and the figure-head revealed. The news flashed round: "It is Miss Morris, Miss Jenny Morris, the one who is sending the *Pride of Wales* gliding smoothly to the sea."

2

A HARD CASE

While the *Pride of Wales* was loading her first cargo at Portmadoc, it became known that she was to sail at once into the sunny seas of prosperity. A long charter under the Indian Government was signed and sealed, and as she sailed blithely through Portmadoc Bay, her proud owner in command, she was waved a long farewell by crowds of fond admirers.

For years the Indian Ocean carried her successfully, and this "pretty model," as she was known out East, brought prestige and credit to her distant home as she bowled along with the regularity of a mailboat between Rangoon and Chittagong. If record pennants were awarded for a ship of her size, she could have claimed a lockerful.

The commander of a large Liverpool full-rigged ship, one Captain Jones, of Bank Place, Portmadoc, told me that in the early 'seventies they sighted a ship in the Indian Ocean. She was wallowing amid spume and spray under a terrific pressure of canvas and moving rapidly through the sea. Twenty-seven sails, ivory white, and fitting like buckram, scooped up the strong breeze of a tropical day. "What ship is that?" asked the Liverpool full-rigger. "J.Q.P.N." (which was the code number of the "Pride of Wales of Portmadoc") came the reply. "What's the hurry, David?" was the next question from the Liverpool ship, followed by her recognition numbers. Both captains came from Portmadoc and were old friends, but had not met for years. There was a friendly wave of the hand as the ships passed on different courses.

Only three of the *Pride of Wales's* original complement saw service in her on this special charter. They were the Captain, the Mate, and Hughes the carpenter who was made boatswain. The fo'c'sle was filled with coolies.

The second in command was a sailor of the old school. He was a very good boxer, too, and this stood him in good stead in the rough-and-tumble life he had to face. He had little use for anyone who called himself a sailor and wasn't one. It is not difficult to visualise the dramas that were enacted on board that little ship during those years of service. The mate's job was a difficult one. He was asked to run a smart ship with human material tragically unequal to the task. As a result, heated words between him and the Captain were frequent. The coolies were signed on for a year. If they happened to be a poor lot and quite unable to stand the strain, they disappeared. If they were defiant and obstinate, they were soon made to bend and obey. The mate was happier with this variety. They at least kept him occupied.

During breakfast one morning when in port, the Captain ventured the sarcastic remark, in view of the fact that everything seemed very quiet on deck: "What time are your men turning-to this *afternoon?*" "There are no bloody men to turn-to, sir," was the Chief's reply. "Where are they?" "They've gone for a long swim." The mate had been among them early that morning, and the crew had escaped over the side in every direction, and had swum ashore for safety, never to return to that ship.

Fifteen years afterwards, when I joined the ship, I was able to read the logs of previous years, and although the entries were laconic they nevertheless proved that the mate had been kept busy, for items read as follows: "*So many of the crew under arrest*"; "*Section of crew mutinied, and ringleaders arrested*"; and so on.

In those days the post of chief or second mate

on a small sailing ship needed no scholar. A pair of good fists were more important than a high navigational qualification, and the mate certainly had these. His hands were much like a wicket keeper's, well knocked about at the joints. After all, these stout fellows were only handing down their heritage. They had to produce men that could stand the acid test of sea-life. The ones I was sorry for were those who had answered the romantic call of the sea and were unable, owing to faint heart or a diseased lung, to react to the case-hardening process, which was severe in the extreme.

There were many ends for these. They could either slip in the rigging and fall on deck, when the remains would be scooped up; or there could be a less ignominious exit by falling off a yard-arm, and becoming a savoury for a shark. "Drowned at sea" always sounded a natural end for a sailor. Several, of course, became pitiable patients for institutions supported by voluntary contributions in all parts of the world. But if the painful jabs of a wisdom tooth breaking through meant anything, many would return home and choose another vocation. I was one of the latter kind.

3

THE TRAMP RETURNS

After many years in the East Indies the *Pride of Wales* sailed for England. She had paid for herself many times over in this while. Having had good fortune with his other ships, although they all had difficult names to live up to, such as the *Success*, *Ocean Monarch*, *Royal Charter*, and *Excelsior*, the owner and commander retired at a very early age.

The new commander, Evan Pugh, sailed the *Pride of Wales* hard for the next ten years and visited every part of the world. In 1887 Captain John Griffith took over the command and held it until she foundered. In 1889 she left Colombo for Havre loaded with coffee, and as she was due for a Lloyd's re-classification in 1890 she returned to her native waters of Portmadoc for the necessary refit.

The ship that I had heard lauded to the skies for her beauty and grace, and to whose thrilling races and exciting experiences I had listened with open mouth, could now be seen from the garden of my home. I must confess that my first impression of her was one of complete disappointment. She looked haggard, battered and worn. Disbelieving my eyes, I raced down to the quay to inspect the *Pride of Wales* from a closer range. All the marine growth and barnacles of two oceans seemed to have stuck to her sides. Her bottle-green timbers were like Joseph's coat of many colours. The gold strake and the elaborate carving round her stern were shabbily tarnished. The beautiful figure-head was sadly in need of a wash and a brush up. Her decks were white enough, but the bulwarks, boats, and deck fittings were more rust than paint.

Twenty years of incessant hammering by the sea was beginning to tell the inevitable tale, of things wearing out, of wrinkles where once there were smiles. In spite of her vagrant appearance, the townspeople gave her a great ovation and welcome. One Evan Lewis, a local carpenter, said she looked the part that only a fine ship could have played, and that some of his physic would soon bring her round.

4

THE CALL OF THE SEA

The refit started in October, and was vigorously continued throughout the winter. By February, 1890, her seams had been entirely recaulked. New parts had been grafted on where necessary. Putty and pitch filled the minor lacerations in her sides. They used to say in those days that old wooden sailing vessels were kept afloat by the three P's: *Putty, Pitch, and Providence.* New copper reached to her loading line. New rigging, spars, and sails brought confidence back in her ability to put up a few more rounds against the demon storm.

A new fo'c'sle was built on deck to replace the squalid dungeon low down in the forepeak. By February 20th, her sailing day, she reminded me of a smartly-dressed middle-aged woman who had been to a beauty specialist to have her face lifted in an endeavour to keep abreast of her younger rivals. However, she captured my imagination and my trust. A certain Dr. Evans came to my help and persuaded my mother that a few voyages through the tropics would build up my frail frame. Captain Griffith, too, was invited home to be wheedled to give me a berth in the cabin, and to be asked to educate me to the sea.

Thus I went to sea instead of going to school. I have often wondered if this was not a good thing to do. Studies seemed to come much easier after seeing a bit of the world. When later I went to school I remember that the boys in the dormitory used to cluster round my bed to hear yarns of the sea. Mine became popular classes, and they were encouraged—but not in the dormitory.

I will now give some details about the ship that was to be my home and mode of transport over many thousands of miles of ocean travel:

THE "PRIDE OF WALES"

Rig	—Three-masted Barque.
Length	—125 feet.
Beam	—26.5 feet.
Draught	—14.5 feet.
Tonnage	—298 register.
Tons	—500 burden.
Deck	—Two, full-sized poop and main-deck.
Cabin	—aft.

Fo'c'sle and galley—abaft the fore-mast.

The freeboard was three feet. This means that, walking along the main-deck amidships, *three feet was the distance to the surface of the sea*, so that it did not do to think too much about that in a storm.

The cabin was cosy. It had mahogany panels with a white ceiling, and a decorative skylight in which hung a tell-tale compass and a swing paraffin lamp and the usual barometer and clock. Leather settees surrounded a mahogany table. There was a snug copper fireplace with a mirror above the mantelpiece. The captain's berth led out on the starboard side. There was an after-cabin which was dark and dingy, lighted only by dead lights. The chief mate's berth led in one direction on the port side, and that of the boatswain and mine in the other. The only light that penetrated these bunks struggled through a small deck dead light. I could not see the foot of my bed except by the aid of artificial light. Lots of things that I had lost used to find their way there.

CHAPTER II

Sailing Day

I

GODSPEED

ON a grey winter morning, in the early 'nineties, Portmadoc harbour presented a scene of unusual activity. The still atmosphere was broken at an early hour by the metallic clank of the dropping pawls of many windlasses. About a dozen ships were preparing for sea. Wives and children and friends of seafaring men were early astir, some taking up their position on a prominent headland known as Pen-y-Banc, from where they waved farewell as the ships, carrying their men-folk, sped past; others clustered in motley gangs at the quayside, to bid godspeed and safe return.

The *Pride of Wales* was the draw on this occasion. Many interested and curious people had congregated at her position. As she had visited the port only once before during her life, and was not likely to come again for at least another seven years, there was reason for the extra demonstration she received. Many people got permission to accompany us over the bar, which was five miles away. Among them were deep-sea men who happened to be home on leave. I must say that gloom and depression had taken charge of my soul—for now that the time had come to cut myself away from my large and jolly family circle and the care of a fond mother, I would have given anything to turn back. But the high spirits and cheerful mood, the bright and breezy demeanour of these tanned and weather-beaten mariners shook me to life; and tailing on to the upper topsail halliard, I pulled my weight to the strains of the rollicking shanty

> *Santa Ana is going away*
> *Away Santa Ana*
> *Santa Ana is going away*
> *Along the planes of Mexico*

The two tug boats, *Snowdon* and *Wave of Life*, were busily dashing up and down the harbour, tugging the ships from the shallower muddy quays and sending them on their way. There was little hope of our floating until the top of the tide. When the *Wave of Life* did come to make fast, there was only a short anchor to get in before the order "Let go the stern rope" was given.

I think most people will agree that there is one thing the Welsh can do—they can sing; and I am sure it will be a long time before I shall feel so stirred as I was on this occasion. The anchor was about to be weighed. Two dozen hardy sailors manned the windlass, and for a quarter of an hour the air of this quaint and secluded harbour was filled with melody. Rich voices, blending in perfect harmony, echoed round those rugged cliffs. Accompanied by the soothing note of dropping pawls, verse after verse of the famous shanty rolled smoothly out of their lusty throats:

> *Blow boys, blow for California O!*
> *There is plenty of gold, so we've been told*
> *On the banks of Sacramento.*

With the order given "Let go the stern rope," we were soon gliding gently away. Three hearty cheers from our friends on shore were vociferously responded to from the poop, where every one had gathered, and with the dipping of the ensign they saw the last of the *Pride of Wales*. We were bound for Germany with 500 tons of slates, the largest single cargo ever taken by a Welsh sailing ship from Portmadoc.

The anxiety of crossing the bar over, the next step was to disembark our visitors to the pilot cutter. Now that we were on the high seas, this did not look too easy, as with main-yards aback, and her stomach filled with slates, the old ship rolled merrily. A buxom woman of rotund dimensions was very difficult to manœuvre over the side, and things became critical when she lost her foot-hold on the none-too-comfortable rope ladder. Fortunately sailors had hold of her wrists, and it was most amusing to see the pilots in the cutter below trying to grab her legs and place her feet on the ladder as they floated out each time the ship rolled in their direction.

Humphrey Owen, our pilot, was now holding matters up. He was nowhere to be found, but presently he emerged from the fo'c'sle, biting his lips to control his emotions. He had been wishing good-bye to his boy of eighteen, who was leaving home for the South Seas for the first time. As I watched the two tugs racing home in time for dinner, tears gushed to my eyes. I gazed vacantly and longingly at that wonderful panorama—the Cambrian range guarded on the right and left by those two silent sentinels, Criccieth and Harlech castles. It was the first time that I realised what a beautiful part of the world I had been living in. I gazed with astonishment at this majestic amphitheatre with Snowdon snow-capped in the centre. Had the distant shores of the Southern Hemisphere anything to equal this scene? Before the question could be answered, the towering seas of the ocean had to be faced, the hurricanes of tropical latitudes encountered, the torrid heat of the equatorial zones endured.

I was now beginning to feel the full effects of the tortures of two of the most distressing maladies that human flesh and mind are heir to—sea-sickness and home-sickness. Climbing into the lifeboat on the main hatch, out of everyone's way, I curled down, caring little what happened. What indescribable despair! And when darkness came, I crawled, frozen and dejected, to my quarters, and sobbed myself to sleep.

There was one thing that I learned that first day at sea, and I never had the occasion to think otherwise. If one is ill or sick in a sailing ship, there is neither the accommodation nor skill to deal with such a contingency. I am not going to say that potions and powders were not administered, for they were, but attention or nursing—no.

I was very glad when I heard that we were making for Falmouth. Our new rigging had got dangerously slack, and there were other minor things that wanted readjusting after a refit. These things could not very well be done at sea. I was immediately impressed by the magnificence of the anchorage and the wonderful harbour of Falmouth. Weaving a way through the outer roadstead, we passed many stately ships calling at Falmouth for orders. Swinging to their anchors and heaving gently to the incoming swell, marine growth on and below the waterline testified a hundred days at sea. Peering over the side in clusters were bronzed and bearded men, meagre of mien, of all ages, with, to me, marvellous blue eyes. I was told that I would look like that in a few months.

Having made several alterations which were suggested after leaving Portmadoc, the most important perhaps being to alter the pitch of the masts, we were anxious to put everything to the test. Leaving Falmouth to a brisk westerly breeze, we were soon moving up Channel in our best stride. The test was now to come. Two vessels that left Wales with us were then able to put up quite a good showing. They had a good start, having left Falmouth two hours earlier. The first one we passed was a schooner called *Ann & Jane Pritchard*. A tougher proposition was the brigantine *George Casson* and the brig *Killia Lass*, but they also fell easy victims. We were next in full cry after a tramp steamer. Although the wind had increased and we were pounding through the sea and spray after her, darkness came to rob us of our joy. Sailors in sailing ships derive much joy and pleasure when a steamer is being passed.

Arriving off the Elbe Light Vessel in the hours of darkness, we were rudely reminded that the river had been frozen over since November, for huge ice floes came crashing against our bows, so huge and closely packed were they that sleep for the watch below was impossible. I was rather disappointed at my first glimpse of Germany. Beacons, a windmill, and the tops of trees were the chief features for quite a long time.

An incident which might have had serious consequences occurred a little later during towing operations. It was very difficult to follow the tug's track accurately, for solid masses of ice would catch a particular bow and throw the ship off her course. However, rounding a buoy rather acutely, we saw a huge wedge of solid ice coming between the tug and ourselves. The ship was going up one cut channel and the tug the other. Almost in a second the tug was seen to be in difficulties. We were, in fact, pulling it over. It appeared that the tow-rope releasing apparatus, owing to the unusual angle, refused to act. The frenzied crew of the tug, yelling wildly and brandishing their arms, were endeavouring to tell us to let go the hawser our end. The rope suddenly broke, to the great relief of the tug and its frightened crew.

2

A GRAND OLD SALT

As soon as it became known that we had been chartered to take a cargo of general merchandise to Rio de Janeiro, a rude shock was in store, for the entire crew from the Chief Mate downwards refused to sign on. This meant that the Captain and myself alone were left. This was too bad, and although Rio's bill of health was always indifferent in those days, it did not quite warrant this drastic decision; for by the time we would be there the worst of the very sickly season would be over. But sailors are like that; much like sheep, they always move in flocks if anything adverse is about in foreign ports. In this instance someone had told them, and this was true, that there were half a dozen large sailing ships in Rio unable to leave because their crew were stricken with yellow fever and smallpox. This report concerned the summer season, Brazil's unhealthiest period.

Strange foreign faces were soon on board— Norwegians, Swedes, and Germans, and a very good lot of men they turned out to be. All excellent sailors, each one had an accordion, and the voyage, whatever else, promised to be musical. They could all muddle along with some sort of English, and were frightfully keen on our shanties. It was very amusing to hear them singing "Blow ze man down, Yonnie, blow ze man down"—they were quite unable to pronounce our "J".

The late 'eighties and the early 'nineties were the peak period of the transition from sail to steam, and it was becoming increasingly difficult to man the cumbersome large sailing ships with the right type of seaman. The turn-over of the old salts, however, was gradual, as many of them preferred to end their days with their old love. But the sailors between eighteen and forty were brought over by the bait of less working hours, with no masts or yards to shin, with regular time for voyages and better pay. No reasonable married man could be expected to refuse £4 10s. a month in steamships as against £3 in sailing ships. It is difficult to know how these men kept wives and families on that amount. Sometimes the wife was allowed to draw half-pay every month, and she would be very lucky if her husband brought any appreciable amount of the other half back at the end of a long voyage.

Little ships like the *Pride of Wales* were preferred by seamen for the simple reason that the work aloft was lighter. I used to watch gangs of

seamen walking about Bute Docks, Cardiff, choos-
ing their ship. They would slink by a four-masted
full-rigged ship, and doing so would cast their eyes
aloft and see a veritable forest of spars—a Chinese
puzzle in ropes. They would then turn up their coat
collars, rub their hands, and double for the first
barque. I was frequently accosted by them in this
manner: "*Where are you bound for in this packet?*"
"*The West Indies.*" "*Ah, that's the spot for me.*"
We scored therefore in that direction as well.

The old salt, too, would become very artful. If
a ship was bound for Valparaiso or 'Frisco, he
would work out where she would be in the winter
season. He would avoid rounding the Horn at the
bad time of year, if instead he could get a ship
going in another direction, say to the East Indies.

In 1895, it was no uncommon sight to see the
remnants of the great sailing ships run by appren-
tices and youths. The nation had by then lost one
of its finest types of manhood. They were a breed
of men of whom the country was proud. There
was no wireless to advertise their fortitude. Their
deeds of valour and suffering perished with them.

I was very lucky to have had the honour of sailing with a typical example of these splendid fellows.
His name was John Davies, his age being then
in the region of seventy. Even at that age he was
worth his weight in gold in any sailing ship. We
were together in the old brig *Excelsior*. John
Davies loved her one day and loathed her the next.
When he was at sea, he despised it. When in
port, he longed for the sea. He had been fifty-five
years afloat. I never heard him say that he liked
any place he had been to—they were either "too
damned hot" or "too damned cold." It was in

a storm that we saw him at his best. It was then that his eyes sparkled the most. Then his personality and presence seemed to radiate a confidence that turned men into supermen. I would say to him: "*I have never seen such terrific seas, Davies. Do you think we are all right?*" And he: "*Well, the old lady (the ship) is boss so far.*" Again: "*Davies, surely this is hurricane force?*" "*Well, I'm not grumbling until the masts are blown out of her.*" That was his way.

Once he and I were sitting yarning on the monkey poop, clad in oilskins, sou'wester and sea boots. All hands had just finished bringing the ship down to snug storm sails. The equinox storm season was at hand. The barometer was so depressed that it had almost assumed the proportions of a grimace. On our weather was an angry-looking horizon. Davies was telling me of the folly of a captain of a full-rigged ship who had disregarded a storm warning, and how the ship was dismasted with the loss of several hands. The howl of the approaching storm and the patter of heavy rain on the sea brought him to a halt. Yelling in my ear, he said: "*It looks as though I shall be able to finish my story in a more realistic atmosphere a little later on. Till then, look after yourself, my lad.*" A terrific storm had struck us.

During one trip in the same ship, the Captain and John Davies were the only persons over eighteen years of age. Davies's displeasure knew no bounds. He hated boys about a ship. From his point of view there wasn't a sailor among them. One day on the high seas, the "kindergarten class," as he called the crew, were actually playing games on the foredeck, games such as tip-and-run and jumping. "*Look at them! Look at them! My God, look at them!*" he entreated the Captain. "*What is the cause of it, Davies?*" asked the latter. "*Cause of it? If you will give these damned children rice pudding for dinner, what can you expect?*" On another occasion one of the boys fell from the rigging, dropping in a heaped mass quite close to the Captain. "*There now,*" was Davies's comment, "*that boy's boot only cleared your head by an inch or two. Haven't I told you, sir, repeatedly, that it isn't safe to walk about the deck this trip?*" One of the youngsters was a farmer's son. It was his first voyage. After a green sea had been shipped, Davies ordered him for'ard to close the fo'c'sle scuttle. The boy looked at him in blank amazement, not knowing a bit what he meant. Davies explained. "*Go and shut the cowshed door, lad, before the calves get drowned.*"

John Davies's best story told against himself is as follows: He was serving on the China Coast in a blue-nose barque, and they were at a port little frequented in those rough sailing days of the 'fifties. He had made some purchases at a certain curio dealer's shop. Later, finding the identical articles at another place in the town marked up at half the price, he was much annoyed and swore revenge. Just before sailing he called at the dealer's again, and by means of signs and wonders suggested that the Chinaman would get much more English business if he showed a sign above his premises appealing for their patronage. The Chinaman was delighted with the idea, and the sign was written and nailed on the premises. Davies invited his shipmates to inspect his handicraft as a signwriter. They were surprised and intensely amused when

c

they read: "Englishmen, keep clear of this ——
rogue." Many years later Davies met a man who
had visited the port since. Davies asked him about
the sign, and was very surprised to learn that the
Chinaman thought it priceless. He, had in fact
given it a much more prominent position. It had
brought the Chinaman a great deal of business,
because it appealed to the Englishman's sense of
humour.

3

A DEEP-SEA GOSPEL

With the advent of the better weather of spring,
I was much looking forward to the run to Rio,
and indulged in day-dreams of wonderful times
and sights in store. I envisaged seeing the south
coast of England at its best, clad in a cloak of new
verdure, passing the many interesting resorts busily
getting ready for their summer season, crossing
the Bay of Biscay, of which I had heard so many
thrilling stories, catching glimpses of the rocky
coast of Portugal, passing through the Forties, to
pick up and run along the chain of pretty islands
on the western shores of Africa, crossing the
Equator, with the attendant ritual of being introduced to Neptune, culminating in sailing along
the Brazilian coast to our destination. How grand!
But disappointment was to come at a very early
date. I had reckoned without the book. I did not
know that creeping round headlands, crawling into
bays, and hugging rocky shores, was a gospel never
preached to the old deep-sea sailing-ship mariner
—his was a conviction deeply rooted that the
quicker he lost sight of land the safer he felt.

Rather different from his brother mariner, the coast-wise sailor who, should he lose sight of land, often felt lost and sometimes was. By this I mean that he was never too sure of his position. Be that as it may, all I saw during the five thousand miles' journey were the terrifying breakers, angrily tossing on the half-covered Goodwins, with stumps of masts sticking up from a recent wreck, a distant view of the twinkling lights of Folkestone, and later the Eddystone Lighthouse.

My introduction to the Bay of Biscay was of an unusually pleasant nature. Escorted by a school of playful porpoises, we sailed blithely through the Bay under ideal conditions, but the long swell of the open ocean was much in evidence, which meant the devil was there, if provoked. I was much impressed at this stage by the entirely changed conditions of the atmosphere and the fresh healthiness of the air. Everything seemed suddenly so pure, so clean, and one threw one's head back to breathe deeper the exhilarating air.

We had during the night plunged, so to speak, from a shelf covered by only a hundred or two fathoms of water into the mighty ocean with its depth of two and a half miles. These shelves, which can be described as the foundation upon which our England stands, extend round the coast to a distance of about a hundred and fifty miles in a westerly direction, or seawards. They act as a gigantic breakwater, for they receive the full force of the huge Atlantic billows which, if they were not thus intercepted and their fury tamed, would alter very considerably the enjoyment and safety of our seaside resorts on the southern and western shores of our islands. For if the sea off Devon and

Cornwall were two miles deep, terrific waves, measuring from two hundred to three hundred yards from crest to crest and towering thirty feet high, whipped by the unbridled tempest, would crash up the English Channel, and the southern coast of England would not be so restful as it is to-day. We found the Forties too as docile as the Bay, and one wondered if that blue sky had ever frowned, or this placid sea ruffled its surface in rage; but we know that some of the worst storms of the Atlantic have been encountered in these latitudes.

Although but a few weeks previous I had, when in the throes of acute nostalgia coupled with devastating attacks of sea-sickness, doubted whether the sea in small sailing ships could, under any conditions or circumstances, offer compensation for such mental and stomachic torture, I soon found that, like other sailors who have short memories for hardships and dangers, my views on the life were slowly changing. My thoughts of home were becoming less distracting, which helped considerably. I now scorned the thought of missing a meal, however capricious the ship's antics might be. I considered this a great victory over the sea, and I soon looked forward to the new life and a new world.

4

A RACE WITH A CLIPPER

We picked up the N.E. trade wind in about a fortnight's time in delightful weather. The Captain seemed determined that the *Pride of Wales* should show his appreciation of the glorious weather by turning her out to look her best. All hands wallowed in *soogie moogie*. Decks were holy-stoned, the mahogany fittings of the quarter deck, heavily ornamented with brass work, were cleaned and varnished. The summer sails, previously bleached by tropical sun, were snowy white, and the ship seemed beautiful enough to be put in a glass case at an exhibition, but her sole admirers were her begrimed and motley crew, and her constant attendant Mother Carey's chicken, lilting merrily in her wake. It seemed odd, when one considered the many sailing ships that must have been in this region, how rarely any were seen. The reason given was that the speed of most square-rigged ships, with the wind dead aft, was much the same, and if by luck they were evenly spaced out at the start, the distance apart would be maintained. Of course, occasionally a clipper would come along and put one to shame, and we experienced this degradation on the same route a year later. I will recount the story now. With break of day, an avalanche of canvas was seen rushing after us, about thirteen miles away. It seems almost incredible that by four o'clock the same day that phantom was out of sight, right ahead, having skimmed past us at midday as if we were at anchor. She was a British full-rigged ship, called the *British Isles*. I heard, some years afterwards, that she had many excellent performances to her credit, but she was never labelled a super clipper.

On another occasion, almost in the same place, we converged with a barque called the *Fortuna*. We kept within sight of each other for ten days in a most amazing manner. Each morning, the *Fortuna* was many miles astern of us, and every evening she was a similar distance ahead. She passed us each day at noon, and we passed her each day at midnight. Signals were exchanged in an endeavour to unravel this mysterious incident, and it was revealed by log readings over the twenty-four hours, that the speed of the *Fortuna* was more or less constant each watch, whereas that of the *Pride of Wales* varied considerably. Although constant over the day watches, she was a knot and a half faster at night. Just before entering the "trades" we had bent an entirely different suit of sails (odd shapes, much worn and well-stretched variety), but good enough for the light winds of the tropics. Under the heavy dew of night, they tautened and became quite respectable fitting sails. The *Fortuna's* constant speed was due to her sails possessing wire bolt ropes so that the dew of the night left them unaffected. Her speed therefore remained constant.

5

"DEAD HORSE DAY"

Dead Horse Day was now close at hand, and as it was always an eventful one in "Jack's" life, a little explanation is necessary here. Sailors are given, at the beginning of a deep-sea voyage, a month's pay in advance. Well, as he spends it in a day, he never reckons he has had it, and contends that for the first month he is working for nothing. Of course, he gets his food, and he thinks in this way he resembles a horse. The last day of the month as a horse, he dies, and once more he becomes a respectable wage-earning human being. Much jubilation naturally runs through the ship, and with some trouble a ceremony is staged. An effigy of an old horse, made out of a tar barrel and old sacks, is dragged along the deck to the break of the poop amid loud cries and groans and boos. Here the Captain and the first mate are invited to the kill. Slinging the old horse outboard, it is set alight, and ceremoniously hoisted towards the main-yard arm to the dirge-like strains of the famous shanty, "The Dead Horse." Soon the halliards catch fire and the burning mass drops into the sea, amid three hearty cheers.

The Captain, in a very agreeable and welcome manner, acknowledges the occasion by inviting all hands to drink his health in a real tot of rum, which as a rule was a treat only to be enjoyed in stormy weather—and a lot of lip-smacking goes on. The sailor loves his grog.

On one occasion, having emerged from the Gulf of Mexico into the Atlantic, just off Key West, we ran into foul weather, and the old ship, loaded with a beastly heavy ore, was straining badly, which necessitated all hands manning the pump almost continuously, waist deep in water. The old man and the cook were waiting to issue a tot when a terrific sea crashed through the fore-rigging, completely filling the decks. A dour sailor remarked, in the midst of all the chaos, danger and discomfort: "If the Old Man doesn't hurry up, we shall have to leave this world with nothing better than salt water on our lips."

6

MY SEA TUTOR

The time was now ripe to start seriously with my seamanship training, for at last possessing a pair of good sea legs and having grasped the importance of the fact that one's life was always in one's own hands, I was able to enter into the daily routine with some confidence.

It was a lucky, and, as well, a happy day for me when the Skipper decided that a Swede called Olaf Ericksen should be entrusted with this responsibility, for Olaf was not only an experienced sailor, having spent twenty years in deep-sea sailing ships, but was the possessor of a kindly heart and a gentle nature, and moreover, being of a communicative disposition, was admirably suited for the job. Sailing many years in British ships, he spoke English quite well, but with the delightful singing Swedish accent of the high-pitched variety. He knew all the shanties through, and saw to it that every one else in the ship knew them. He would sit on the main hatch during the dog watch, balancing an accordion on his knee and reel them off, one after the other, many times over. He would meticulously correct any one not quite sure of the right words, and this method of doing everything correctly was applied to the execution of his work.

There was little he did not know of ocean life, and however important the subject of his teaching might be, his blue eyes were always on the alert to pick up something extra that was interesting to tell me in this wondrous realm through which we were passing. Every day brought fresh charms and revelations to thrill a young life.

7

FLYING FISH

Arriving suddenly in the domain of the flying fish, a day filled with excitement was in store, and as it was Sunday every advantage could be taken to enjoy it. Below watch went by the board, and all hands were feverishly engaged in preparing for the feast. Fishing tackle, spears, harpoons, and nets were put through a rapid overhaul. For the first time since leaving home, this day found my mind awakened by the actual realities of some of those stirring and thrilling stories that we used to listen to round the winter hearth. The stage was set for what was to be a scene of unusual magnificence, and one would have to visit the tropics a good many times to get so excellent an opportunity of studying the habits of some of the most beautiful and interesting fish that are known to man.

A brilliant sun shone from a cloudless sky, the surface of a transparent sea was scarcely ruffled by the slightest of breezes, and we seemed to have arrived in the centre of a vast arena, where a great display had been arranged especially for our benefit.

When a school of hungry dolphins settle down to their favourite lunch, the flying fish, then the hunt is grand; for both are exceedingly speedy, and as the flying fish can resort to the air when cornered, the deck of an old wind-jammer makes an excellent Royal Box from which the antics of that most beautiful of all fish—the Dolphin—making his gracefully-curved leaps into the air after his quarry, can be seen in detail.

The flying fish has a very hard life, and being such a dainty and tasty morsel he is much in demand as an article of diet, with the result that he is persecuted not only by other fish night and day but also by birds, when he deigns to take to the air, where he hopes to be out of harm's way just for a brief moment or two. The flying fish is about the size of a small or medium mackerel, and in addition to the usual fins for propelling him in the sea he possesses a pair of long wings which fold neatly into his sides. When he breaks surface, then the wings come into action and off he goes at terrific speed. He rarely rises higher than is necessary to keep him out of harm's way— anything up to twenty feet. He can turn, rise or fall with ease and rapidity, and can remain in the air long enough to cover a distance of about half a mile or so. But as soon as his wings are dry, the flight is over.

It is interesting to see a large school manœuvring gracefully in the air, then suddenly there is a flop, a splash, and they are out of sight! So continuously harassed is the flying fish that he has but little time to look around for food, and is apparently driven to barbaric extreme, for he is frequently found guilty of devouring the junior members of his own family. We proved this a voyage or two later when we caught a shark. Inside the shark was a full-sized dolphin. This was a strange discovery, for, with his great speed, a dolphin can usually make rings round a shark; but he must have been caught unawares.

A similar operation on the dolphin revealed many flying fish. A further operation on the flying fish proved this case. At night the disturbed shoals

fly into the track of the ship and many collide
with rigging and sails and drop on deck. The
flapping of their wings reveals their location, and
a race ensues towards them between the crew and
the ship's cats. We also, like the dolphin, thought
this fish very good eating, and their infrequent
visits were always eagerly welcomed by the crew.

The dolphin's colour schemes are seen at their
best as he twists and twirls in his chase of the flying
fish. In action his basic colours of bright flame
and rich peacock blue are thrilling to behold as
they blaze in the sunlight. In the dolphin's more
sober moods the iridescence of the flame and blue
is more subdued. When in full cry, as many as
half a dozen dolphin at a time may be seen leaping
in the air, and they make one think of some mysterious hand throwing crescent settings of brilliants
from the seas, so dazzling is the effect.

The dolphin, like a good many other deep-sea
fish, is most companionable, and he will fuss round
a sailing ship in an amazing manner. It seems a
pity in these days of fashionable travel that these
experiences are completely denied those who go
in steamships, for the speed, the hurry, the churning
propellers and the continuous vomiting of ashes
and refuse oil into his pure realm, is most distaste-
ful to the dolphin, and he turns away in disgust.

8

GRAND ESCORT OF DOLPHIN

When their lunch of flying fish was over, the
school hurried to pay us a visit, and the curtain
was raised on a thrilling and most beautifully-

staged second act. Some of us clambered on to
the guys of the jib-boom that run through the
martingale, a spar known as the dolphin striker,
from where could be best observed a scene of
unparalleled charm. The ship was completely
surrounded by dolphin and bonito, and as the sea
was very calm it was possible to see the ship's
underwater sides right down to the keel. Even
lower than that fish could be seen nosing their
way through the others for the honour of gently
brushing against the ship's side. Dolphins and
bonitos vied with each other for pride of position
and ceremoniously changed places in the grand
escort as we moved slowly along.

Many fish, measuring from two to four feet,
were caught both with line and spear, and without any apparent concern or chagrin to the others,
for they remained calm and undisturbed. The
dolphin possesses a white flesh with a delicate
flavour, but sailors eat it with a certain amount
of fear, as poisoning cases have been known.
Sailors, however, will run the risk; and they enjoy
the change that these days bring from the ever-
lasting salt beef and pork diet. The bonito, where
there is nothing else better to be had, also enters
into the sailor's diet, but to tackle a bonito steak
requires a man possessed of a resolute digestion
and the jaws of a shark.

CHAPTER III

THE TERRORS OF CALM

I

A ROLLING SHIP

ONE day I was throwing a ball of spun yarn for Olaf while he was serving a rope with the usual serving mallet, Stockholm tar and grease, when he asked me to stand upright in the middle of the deck and look for my shadow. The sun shone brilliantly, but I searched in vain for my shadow. Olaf laughed and explained. The sun was absolutely and directly overhead. It was my first mid-summer day in the tropics, and one that I shall have cause ever to remember. It was the beginning of a week of the utmost discomfort and torture. We were becalmed. Our faithful friend the trade wind had deserted us. It should have carried us on some hundreds of miles further south. This caused the Captain some concern. Had a bad course been steered during the night, which had taken us too much eastward? Our position was determined under great difficulty, for the violent rolling made it difficult to keep a good horizon. It was discovered that we were a bit out. Of all the disagreeable conditions at sea in sailing ships, perhaps being becalmed is the most unhappy. One is immediately obsessed with a feeling of extreme hopelessness and helplessness. Although

45

most of the calm patches of a permanent nature in the oceans are defined and known to navigators, nevertheless it is possible, when skirting these areas, even allowing a good margin of safety, to strike a calm patch. There we were, one of the unlucky ones; and there we remained for many days.

As far as the eye could see, the ocean resembled an oily barren waste, bereft of colour or character, heaving listlessly in huge crestless billows. We were now rolling as no ship could ever have rolled before, and the terrific flapping of the sails with each roll made it necessary to haul up and lower all the heavy canvas and to furl the lighter royals and top-gallant sails. This latter duty usually devolved on the lesser experienced members of the crew, but on this occasion it became a man's job. The roll of a ship, when ungoverned by wind resistance, is unmercifully violent; and to be hurled through the air many times a minute, a hundred feet above the sea, poised on a slender stretch of rope attached to a flimsy spar, calls for a man possessed of a stout heart and a seasoned digestion, remembering that he has something to do besides looking after his own safety. Even these stalwart Scandinavians returned to deck looking green about the gills, indicating that they felt the effects of a nerve-racking experience.

It was a grim spectacle to see a sailing ship in mid ocean with no sails set. Life was becoming hourly more difficult and unbearable, and cooking was already almost out of the question. With great difficulty, small relays of water could be boiled to make tea and coffee, cracker hash, a dish made from broken-up biscuits and chopped-up beef or

pork, to form a sort of baked pie, was the height
of the cook's culinary achievements. To move
about the ship, one had to crawl from one rope
to another—legs were useless. The usual routine
work had to be abandoned, as two hands were
necessary to hang on. Hammocks had to be sub-
stituted for bunks; it was impossible to sleep in
the latter, as the whole of one's internals seemed
to jerk from one side to the other. This was dread-
fully unpleasant, and the operation went on twelve
times every minute, 700 times an hour, and sixteen
thousand times a day, and for six dreary days.
Some of the rolls were so heavy that the vessel
scooped the sea over both sides and filled the decks.

The heat of the sun was unbearable during most of
the day; and after the fourth day I was, with one or
two more of the less experienced sailors, beginning
to feel sick from the constant reflection of a relentless sun on this mirrored expanse. One's half-
closed eyes ached, the decks were so hot, except
where deck wash rushed to and fro, that the pitch
bubbled out of the seams. Much anxiety was felt
as time went on for the safety of the masts, as the
rigging was becoming dangerously slack. With
each roll the rigging and stays tautened with an
ominous "ping." Measures had to be taken to rig
all the support possible in the form of spare tackle,
to ease the terrific strain.

*The masts and sails of two sailing ships bound
south could be seen, serenely enjoying a nice breeze
about fifteen miles away, but they did not see our
limp signal.* We were now in our sixth day; and
conditions were much worse because the hull of
the ship was showing signs of strain, and the
pumps had to be attended to frequently. Late

that day a puff of smoke was seen on the horizon; shortly the hull of a large steamer hove in sight, but as she was steering an oblique course she was not likely to come much closer. However, to our frantic joy, she appeared suddenly to change course. Yes, she was making for us. Our strange appearance had attracted her attention. Wonders on the deep never cease. Suddenly when she was five miles away, a gentle ripple broke over the oily surface of the sea. A heaven-sent breeze had reached us, and by the time the large French emigrant ship, called the *Uruguay*, bound from Marseilles to the River Plate, had reached our position, our sails were filled with the most welcome breeze that ever blew. Hundreds of emigrants crowded to the side to give us a hearty cheer, and a blast from her siren wished us good night. It seemed that we had been awakened from a horrible nightmare.

I often have wondered whether the *Uruguay's* change of course had in any magic or scientific way influenced the breeze towards us—so uncanny did it seem, that it reminded one of a brougham bringing the doctor to one's door. Whichever way it was, we looked upon her as our deliverer, and that in spite of the breeze arriving first. We afterwards felt sorry, in our anxiety and excitement to set every sail, that darkness came before we had time to collect our thoughts to run up a signal of thanks for the amiable gesture she had made in closing on us. Anxiously cleaving our way in the wake of the *Uruguay's* massive hull, her twinkling stern light occasionally hidden by clouds of black smoke belching from her funnel, we were the happiest ten souls in all the world!

The immense rolling that we had experienced, and which had caused us such distress and discomfort, was mainly due to the nature of our cargo, about a third of which was exceedingly heavy material, placed lowermost in the hold; the lighter merchandise of many hundreds of packing cases containing matches, musical instruments, such as pianos, etc., occupying the remainder of the space as far as the deck line. The result was that the ship resembled the pendulum of a grandfather clock with the weight at the lower end, and producing the same action, tick-tock, which was only countered when the breeze filled our sails.

2

ERICK'S STORY

A seaman who went by the name of Erick, who was on the starboard watch, and owing to his prowess with the sailing needle was excused in the tropics all other routine duties so that he could get on with the sail-making job, told me some harrowing and gruesome experiences that befell him and his companions in a big ship when she was becalmed for two long periods during the same passage. I used to spend a lot of my time talking to Erick—he was so interesting and such an experienced seaman. Sitting on the other end of his form, and watching him deftly wielding a clumsy needle through canvas the thickness of leather with the rapidity of a seamstress, was intriguing.

The story was that they were homeward bound from 'Frisco and experienced light weather almost all the way. This goes to show that it is not always

D

necessary to be knocked about by heavy seas, or to be blown to bits by gales and hurricanes, to court disaster in a sailing ship. They were three weeks becalmed in the Pacific, which meant that the passage home could be nothing better than about a hundred and forty days; and before they encountered the second bout of calm, symptoms of that dreadful scourge, scurvy, were evident all through the ship. The men's teeth were becoming loose and their flesh pappy. Then the second lot of bad luck came, not very far from where we were at that moment. This was at a point somewhere north of the line, and it lasted for three weeks. It was long enough to kill many of the brave fellows, who might have been saved had this second calamity been averted. Shortage of fresh water, poor rations, lack of medical skill and appliances and virtually no nursing, bring about appalling conditions.

When they did eventually arrive in the Channel it was with the greatest effort that they mustered enough strength among those who could stand to drop the anchor. Similar experiences were frequent; both Queenstown and Falmouth could tell blood-curdling tales of a sailor's life in long-distance sailing ships during the greater part of the nineteenth century. Erick's health had never recovered; he was always pale and emaciated, and all his teeth, with the exception of three or four in odd places, had fallen out, which made it necessary to put his old hard biscuit in a canvas bag and smash it to crumbs with a hammer before he could eat it. He found it difficult to chew tobacco, and had to hold his pipe continuously with his hand to enjoy a smoke. He never grumbled.

3

IN THE DOLDRUMS

Two days later we ran into another calm, but on this occasion it presaged our arrival in the doldrums, where sunshine and storm alternately frolic. Heavy squalls, accompanied by torrential rain and terrifying thunderstorms, hold the stage a while; then a sudden change to delightful conditions of summer weather. These strange climatic conditions continue for hundreds of miles, and to weave through them until the trade winds south of the Equator are met means a strenuous time for all hands. The sudden, and often violent gusts, coming from any and every direction, keep the watch on tenterhooks, particularly at night, when their approach is most difficult to detect. It becomes necessary to indulge in varied manœuvres of seamanship in order to keep on level terms with these freakish conditions; staying, wearing, box-hauling ship, shortening canvas and setting it again in double-quick time, is the order of the day. On occasion many of these squalls can be counted within one's immediate vision. They move in angry-looking storm formations, each clump carrying its own thunder and lightning, besides its other disagreeable components. I have heard some people say that they enjoy a thunderstorm and are particularly thrilled with heavy lightning. To these people I strongly recommend a visit to the doldrums in a sailing ship, for here they get that prolonged flash which illuminates with that ghastly bluish effect of blinding intensity. Local atmosphere, in the form of a tropical deluge which compels one to come to a standstill to gasp for breath, incessant roll of terrifying thunder, accompanied quite occasionally by wind of hurricane violence, and a cross turbulent sea, should come up to their expectations of a good performance.

Emerging from one of these squalls into brilliant sunshine, I saw a marvellous sight. There were two four-masted ships racing along with lee rails awash. They were both the worse for wear, for they had lost some sails, but it did not seem to matter. Our Skipper drily remarked: "Any fool can set a sail, but it takes a sailor to stow one." Their cloud of snow-white sails stood out in pleasant and refreshing relief against the angry lightning-streaked background. Dark clouds have silver linings indeed, so particularly welcome at this stage is the delightful rain that quickly fills the deck.

Water economy is always rigidly observed in deep-sea sailing ships; tank capacity is worked out with little to spare for any other purpose beyond what is necessary for cooking and thirst-quenching purposes. On these harvest occasions it was only necessary to plug the scuppers to find the deck covered to a depth of a foot with deliciously refreshing rain water. Sparsely clad, bearded and be-grimed sailors swarmed the deck, each carrying a poverty-stricken parcel of clothing, a bar of soap, and shaving utensils.

For the next twelve hours the decks resembled the drying grounds of a laundry—wherever one went one had to dodge a shirt. Men, whose bearded and dirty faces had given them the air of being hardy, experienced, and weather-beaten, now that they had washed and shaved looked simpering and youthful.

Hans, a young fair-haired, round-featured Swede, of ordinary seaman rank, whose face had hitherto looked like a full moon embroidered with a flaxen growth of down, now looked like a buxom and blushing dairymaid, whereas his pal Gustav, a dark pallid long-faced variety of the same race, had developed, through a desire to economise water, an apostolic-looking countenance; now that he had shaved he resembled a gigolo, for he had left a portion of his whiskers on each cheek bone. The most noticeable improvement, if such a term can be applied, was to be seen in the case of the boatswain, a good-natured, gruff-voiced man of short stature and rotund development, hailing from Altona. He took well to the bath, and came through the ordeal minus a blob of tar that had been on his cheek for several days, and without a very bristly beard. We missed the beard. It was fascinating to watch it when the boatswain was angry. One corner of his mouth then dropped, and all the bristles of his beard shot in the same direction.

4

"CRACKING ON"

Making good progress from squall to squall, the Equator could not now be very far away. The Polar star and other familiar groups were no longer visible, but legions of others had come up to fill the new heaven under which we were now sailing. Set in a maze of stars of lesser brilliance shone conspicuously the formation known as the Southern Cross, and as our jib-boom played between its stars, it seemed to attract us and welcome us to the Southern Hemisphere.

Many sailing ships were now seen, all making for the same spot on the Equator where the most favourable conditions can be found for crossing. Homeward-bound and outward-bound ships here met, and exchanged friendly greetings. Clippers still eager for records dashed by under a cloud of canvas, whereas the older ships, with worn gear and sails, took things more sedately.

Life on a clipper is hard and hazardous and full of anxiety. I know of nothing more nerve-racking than to be on a sailing ship that is carrying more canvas in heavy weather than she is reasonably expected to do. I remember being caught on a lee shore in a small West India trader, and the thought of the experience, although it happened so long ago, even now quickens my pulse. The ship was a two hundred-ton brig called the *Excelsior*, loaded down to hatches with a heavy mineral. We had rounded Land's End, with little to spare, and were steering a course up the Irish Sea before a fresh south-wester and making excellent progress, when in a twinkling the wind flew round to north-west, and instantly increased to gale force. We were caught in a cleft stick, a raging storm on one side, and the inhospitable coast of Cornwall with its towering bleak cliffs, rising perpendicularly to a height of three hundred feet, on the other. Although a sailor loathes a lee shore, he does cling to a shadow of hope, if the worst comes, that he might be hurled into a cleft or crevice, or a friendly coastguard might fire a rocket at him, and haul him to safety. No evidence fostering such a hope brought comfort to our souls

on this occasion—the only visible signs that life
was about were a couple of gaunt, gale-swept
shafts of tin mines. The Captain, an experienced
mariner, resolved to pit the strength of his frail
craft against the storm. This meant driving the
ship under an abnormal pressure of canvas against
the onslaught of the terrific seas, so as to eliminate
as far as possible any drift or leeway towards the
shore and hope that everything would hold, and
that we might last the gale out and keep a weather
position. This, by performing Machiavellian feats
of seamanship, we did.

Looking back on that occasion now, I must say it
was a wonderful sight to see those eight shrivelled
souls, lashed to a row of belaying pins, watching
in agonised tension every move and quiver of their
little ship as she gamely battled against the gale.
She was magnificent. Upper topsails, lower topsails, foresail, mainsail, fore topmast staysail and
reefed trisail, sent her crashing against the mountainous sea (and they are mountainous just there);
sheets of blinding sea and spray shot high over
the main top gallant yard, eighty feet above the
deck. It was a most nerve-racking experience.
At last I knew what "lee sheer poles awash"
meant.

I determined to finish with the sea after that
experience. In this instance, the foolhardy practice of "cracking on" as they call it was an extreme
measure in a critical situation; but the old tea
clippers frequently indulged in the performance,
just for the sake of knocking a day or two off a
record, or of winning a tea race. Of course it
must be remembered that their special ships were
issued with the best and strongest equipment,

regardless of cost. This adds greatly to the mariner's confidence and governs the amount of risk he can afford to take.

5

RIO AT LAST

Now to return to sunnier climes. It was apparent from dead reckoning that we should be crossing the Equator in the small hours of the morning. No demonstration had been arranged, in spite of the fact that Hans, Gustav, and myself were due for a christening at the hands of Father Neptune, and that we were looking forward to the pleasure of being introduced to the charming sea goddess Amphitrite, and their entourage. However, the Captain very graciously stepped into the breach and paid us the compliment of staying up until eight bells (midnight). He also issued rum rations to all hands to mark the occasion. This seemed to suit every one's taste and was much appreciated.

That night in the middle watch, Olaf tattooed an anchor on my arm to commemorate the crossing. The ingredients and implement were primitive; a piece of coal reduced to powder and made into paste with water, and a sailing needle. The operating theatre was the cook's galley, dimly lighted by a naked wick flame of a colza oil lamp. However, everything worked well, and the anchor is still on my arm.

Finding the south-east trade in the correct place and in a particularly fresh mood, the remaining thousand miles were polished off in about a week; and we arrived at Rio's latitude fifty-seven days after leaving the Elbe, which was not bad going, considering the very light weather we had enjoyed almost all the way and the wasted days when we were becalmed. When I went below at eight o'clock in the morning there was nothing in sight, but one could instinctively smell that there was land somewhere near. However, coming on watch again at noon, there was a marvellous surprise waiting for me. A wonderful range of curiously-shaped mountains could be seen on the starboard bow only about twenty miles away. I scampered about the deck in feverish excitement, talking to everyone. I rushed down to the cabin, where the Captain was engaged in working out the ship's noonday position, and shot at him a volley of questions—questions that only an excited youth would ask, and be forgiven for asking.

The fact of the matter was, I had become so accustomed to the dreariness of the ocean that it would not have surprised me much if I had never seen land again, and at times I was obsessed with the idea that I should not. Then suddenly to find it, what joy! "South America!" the Captain exclaimed. "Those mountains form a part of the Brazilian coast;" and pointing to a smooth cone-shaped formation superimposed against the great range, "that is the famous Sugar Loaf mountain, and marks the entrance to the most beautiful harbour in the world. But unless some wind comes from somewhere we shall never get there!"

We were again becalmed. I was impressed by the peculiar shape of the high peaks; they appeared to have been artificially finished off. Some were smooth, some angular, others rounded off in strange shapes and designs, giving the impression that trowel and mortar had been used to fill up the crags and crevices, and smooth them over. They were very unlike our Welsh mountains.

During the afternoon we were busily engaged getting the anchors outboard, hauling up the cable chains and swinging the boats into the davits, and making general preparations for port. A large tug-boat called the *Emperor* paid us a visit, and seemed very desirous of taking us in tow. It was amusing to hear the tug's dark-skinned skipper, immaculately dressed in white ducks and covered with gold braid, gradually working up through a general conversation in very broken English to the price he intended to ask for the tow, and the least he was prepared to accept. He would attempt to flatter when no response was made to his price. "Ah, Captain, she ees a beeg sheep, isn't eet?" However, our Welsh price did not please him, and as he rang "full speed ahead" on his engines, he waved his benedictions and ejaculated a short phrase in a foreign tongue, containing many sacros.

One felt sorry for the Captain, undergoing this gruelling ordeal in the presence of his crew, who of course thought he was mean not to accept the tug's lowest figure. It is difficult to conceive anything so completely successful in taking the pomp out of a Captain's quarter-deck strut as the harangue of a tug-boat's skipper, particularly when the dialogue takes place in a calm, an occasion when a sailing ship looks silly.

Soon after sunset, a refreshing breeze sprang from an easterly direction, and hopes of spending that night, after all, tucked up in a steady bunk in a snug harbour were revived. Joining Erick, who was posted for "look-out" duties on the fo'c'sle head, we walked to and fro chatting about Rio, often spellbound by the majesty of those strangely-fashioned peaks as they rose higher and higher into the starlit heaven. Erick knew the place well, and said I was extremely fortunate in having the unusual opportunity of sailing into the port for the first time during the hours of darkness, as it was considered to be one of the things to do— although, in reality, it is never dark in the true sense of the word, unless there happens to be a mist about. The cloudless sky, filled with twinkling stars, the clean and clear atmosphere, enabled us to follow the great ranges as they towered above and girdled the silent water of this sublime harbour.

Soon after nine that night, the *Pride of Wales* had arrived at the imposing portals of Rio de Janeiro, and the glow of the lights of the great city illuminated the sky for miles around. We had covered in the region of six thousand miles in fifty-nine days without seeing any land, and during that period (except of course the queer storms of the doldrums) we had enjoyed just heavenly weather.

CHAPTER IV

Round About Rio

BOMBARDMENT

JUST about this time, Brazil was in a very unsettled state. A civil revolution had recently deposed the monarch, Don Pedro II, and with his downfall the rule of the House of Braganza ended. A republic had been proclaimed, and the country was slowly settling down, but still a good deal of nervousness existed, particularly during the hours of darkness, lest someone should attempt to restore the monarchy, or to institute some other form of government.

Before we left Hamburg we were given to understand that possibly the entrance to Rio, the Federal capital, would be closely guarded, and vessels making the port, particularly between sunset and sunrise, would be subjected to a close examination and would have to take care to obey all the regulations, though these were issued and re-issued with frequency.

Arriving at a position between the two entrance forts, we rather expected to be intercepted by a boarding vessel, which would go through the usual routine of examination; but nothing happened of this kind. Instead we were merely challenged by a gruff voice through a megaphone, which hurled at us a jumble of foreign words. We replied by yelling the name of the ship and the port of departure, which to them must also have been a jumble of perfectly unintelligible foreign words, for within a few seconds the graceful and celestial surroundings were rudely shaken by the booming of guns—the battery had opened fire on us! My God! what had we done? What could we do to prove that we were an innocent merchantman?

There were no signs that we had come to any harm, but we were terrified beyond description. We crouched under cover of deck fittings, too frightened to move. We eventually mustered enough courage to come into the open to execute belated and half-hearted orders. The top gallant sails were lowered, courses hauled up and the ship brought into the wind, and main-yards backed. Whether this manœuvre was interpreted by the garrison as an acceptance of their challenge or not I did not know, but it brought forth more firing, this time from another fort, nearer in. The explosions were terrifying to a degree, but we did not appear to be sinking. What did it all mean? If they were blank shots, would the next one be a live round?

However, out of the filth and commotion shot two pinnaces, filled with people of the swashbuckle type, some carrying arms, others hurricane lamps. They bumped alongside in a most brusque and unseamanlike manner, scrambled into the rigging and rushed the deck. We fled in every direction to hide. They eventually made for the poop, and there found the Captain, with whom they remonstrated in a forcible manner, gesticulating wildly between strange and incomprehensible utterances.

Having been shown over the ship and having examined the papers, things quietened down considerably, and the Captain was made to understand that he had omitted to carry out the necessary instructions for entering the port after sunset. He was told that he could be summoned for the offence and heavily fined, but as amendments to regulations had been issued while we were on the high seas he was acquitted of any misdemeanour.

2

RIO HARBOUR

With the departure of our unwelcome visitors the displeasing interlude was forgotten and our frayed nerves quickly recovered their normal composure. Weaving our way wearily towards the anchorage, we were abreast of the great city which was a blaze of illuminations. These, together with the riding lights of many ships in the bay, seemed to surround us with confusion; we had neither a tug-boat nor a pilot, and with a fast-falling wind it must have been a most difficult task for the Captain to get us in. However, we passed between two large sailing ships, and found ourselves in a forest of shipping.

We were forced to "come to" in a poor berth which gave us little clearance, when swinging, from fouling several vessels. We were close to a large four-masted ship whose bows towered above our stern. We could hear a group of her sailors, who had apparently been disturbed by the firing, alluding to us as "the little blighter that caused all the bother." We now scampered aloft in

detached parties to make fast the sails. Olaf and
I were detailed to the fore top-gallant sail, and
for the first time I was entrusted to take charge
of my own yard-arm—quite a responsibility—and
I felt a real sailor.

What a wonderful sight met our gaze as we
stood in the cross trees, a hundred feet above the
sea. Stretching from the foot of the Sugar Loaf
mountain were festoons of twinkling lights
illuminating the graceful curves of the foreshore
and the gay promenades, each one throwing a
reflection on the shimmering sea. Towards the
centre of the city they rose in symmetrical tiers,
right up the mountain slopes and extended for
miles to the north-west, and disappeared in the
distant shadows. To me it was the fairy land of
my dreams.

All round, on the still water rode half a hundred
large sailing ships of every conceivable rig. What
a feast of joyous excitement the morrow would
bring! With the coiling of the last rope came a
welcome respite. There was one thing that we
missed, namely the invigorating air of the open
ocean, which for two months had kept us toned
to a high pitch of physical fitness. Its place had
suddenly been taken by a warm breeze that swept
the sun-scorched mountains, laden with a delicious
aroma of pine and mellow fruit and spice, followed
by fickle wafts of oppressive air that seemed to
have percolated through the narrow streets, collecting in its course disagreeable reminders of
congested thoroughfares, busy market centres, and
poor sanitation.

Thus ended an exciting day and an eventful
passage. We went below to rest our tired limbs,

possessed of the precious thought that on this
occasion no rude hand would shake one's shoulders, nor a vulgar voice disturb one's peaceful
slumber at that unwholesome hour of four in the
morning. Breakfast for all hands was to be at
eight.

A great deal has been written and spoken about
the wonderful harbour of Rio. You will always
hear sailors arguing as to the respective merits of
Rio's harbour and that of Sydney in Australia.
My view is that when the harbours of this world
are boiled down to two, then it surely does not
matter much which is the finer.

When I came on deck the following morning
and took a cursory glance round the compass, my
impression was, "This must be heaven!"

We were not allowed to remain more than a
day in the original anchorage. Our new berth
appeared to be much nearer the city, which was
much more pleasing, as we were not shut in by
innumerable ships. From this point we could
watch the active life of the great city without the
aid of binoculars, and the panorama was superb.

During the process of towing, we passed several
magnificent sailing ships. All the "Marions of
Scotland" seemed to have foregathered here. The
four-masted full-rigged ships included the beautiful
Trafalgar, the *Pegasus*, *Afghanistan*, and *Marion
Lightbody*. There were also there the four-masted
barque *Puritan*, the full-rigged ships *Marion Inglis*,
Marion Ballatine, and *Corby*, and the large iron
barques *Maelgwyn* and *Savernake*.

Rio in those days, the early 'nineties, was beginning in a very resolute manner to modernise and
improve its sanitary schemes, which had up to

this time left much to be desired. It was notoriously unhealthy, particularly in the hottest season. Small-pox and yellow fever exacted a heavy toll of life annually, and every one who lived there or who visited the place seemed equally liable to fall before either of these dreaded scourges. There was hardly one native over forty years of age whose face did not carry the pitted evidence of smallpox. When we arrived, two English vessels had only just cleared the port, where they had been marooned for months, stripped of almost every member of their crew owing to smallpox and yellow fever. However, great praise is due to the authorities for the whole-hearted and determined manner in which they set about the job of cleaning up the port.

Almost all the English ships were filled with contrivances to improve sanitation, and, within a few years, they had succeeded in stamping out this ghastly state of affairs, so that by the beginning of the twentieth century Rio could claim to be among the world's healthiest cities.

3

GRAND VIEW

The entrance to Rio is in reality an imposing gorge, which breaks the continuity of the coastal mountain range which we had seen to such exquisite advantage from twenty-five miles out at sea. It is guarded on each side by sentinel peaks, the one on the left side being peculiarly attractive, for it possesses a most fantastic shape (as can be seen in the plate), and rises abruptly to a height of over a thousand feet. It is called the Sugar Loaf (Pao de Assucar), and looks quite impossible to climb, but I believe some English sailors once did climb to the summit. To-day, an aerial tram takes people in stages right up to the top, and they say the view is incomparable. This huge granite cone provides the navigator with an excellent landmark. On the starboard side are steep characteristic cliffs of impressive grandeur. Their smooth sides run right down to the sea, but the monotony is broken by an interspersion of large groups of palm trees and tropical vegetation of vivid green, which produce an inspiring effect. The fort which fired at us lies at the foot of the Sugar Loaf.

Immediately the entrance is made, which is about a mile from shore to shore, a view of great magnificence meets the eye. The whole circumference of this majestic and superb land-locked bay opens out, and it extends towards the high mountains at the back for a distance of about fifteen miles, and the breadth varies from three to eight miles. It is studded with innumerable little islands, each covered with a green mantle, while delightful chalets, with coloured roofs, peep out between the shady branches of palm trees.

The bay by day and by night presents animated and gay scenes. Scores of awninged pleasure craft and ferry boats, throwing their white shadows on the calm sea, constantly thread their way through clusters of stately sailing ships and ocean liners.

Although the city lies to the south side, there are charming suburbs dotted here and there in the bay which can be reached much more pleasantly and just as quickly by ferry boat. The most important, perhaps, is Nictheroy, about four to five miles immediately opposite the main city. Here the well-to-do inhabitants of Rio rush to find relaxation and rest from the oppressive and busy atmosphere of the great town. Nictheroy possesses a delightful beach admirably suited for bathing, boating, and yachting. The ferry boat to Nictheroy is always well patronised, but the rich merchants of Rio make the crossing in luxuriously-appointed private launches.

What strikes one particularly about the whole place is the fact that all the buildings, houses, and promenades are white, and therefore most attractive, for they make a fascinating contrast with the darker natural surroundings. From the centre of two ridges rises a tall rugged mountain, called the Corcovado (Hunch Back), to a height of over two thousand feet. Buildings are scattered on the slopes and climb high up the mountain side until the gradient becomes too steep. A magnificent view of Rio is to be seen from the heights of Corcovado.

4

THE BUMBOAT AND THE DEAD BOAT

The first time we landed at the harbour steps, I happened to be a member of the boat's crew, and when in the act of unshipping the rudder I was amazed to hear my name being called. On looking round I saw a young Welsh fellow whom I seemed to know quite well standing on the quay. He was none other than a member of our crew who had sailed with us from Portmadoc, but who had left with the others at Hamburg. His name was Richard Owen, the son of the pilot who had taken us over Portmadoc Bar. He was apparently determined to come south, and had joined the Welsh iron barque called the *Maelgwyn*. He was much changed. He had grown fatter, and the tropical sun had brought many freckles to his face.

Although we were moored half a mile from the shore, we were never dull, because there was always so much small shipping and pleasure craft passing that one was kept both amused and interested. Frequent visits were paid to our ship by those little floating shops known to sailors as "bumboats," some tastefully displaying locally-made trinkets, others filled with cages of chirping tropical birds of infinite variety and brilliant plumage, while others were elaborately and daintily laid-out fruit stalls, which scented the air deliciously.

The owners scull the bumboats from ship to ship, and Rio without its bumboats would lose one of its attractive features. The enterprising owner is a most good-natured fellow, for he has to stand up to a lot of back-chat and stiff bargaining at the hands of sailors before he can hope to bring off a deal, however small. The strange thing was that he never seemed to take any money; at least, he rarely seemed to get any. An old shirt, or a pair of very old trousers long past the stage of respectability tolerated even in sailing ships, would weigh down many bananas and oranges, or procure a voluble parrot.

I used to spend most of my week-ends sailing in the bay, and encircling those enchanted islands. I never had any difficulty in finding sailors to accompany me. This was very necessary, as during parts of the day there never was too much wind. It invariably meant getting down to the oars to regain the ship.

On one occasion we went as far as Nictheroy, which was a delightful sail and most interesting. As we approached the shore, many bathers swam out and rested on our gunwhale. The young Portuguese girls are exceedingly pretty. They all possess gleaming white teeth, and as their skins are bronzed, with jet-black hair, they have a characteristic expression which is full of seductive charm, and their smile is meltingly attractive. Nictheroy was seething with gaiety, and the little town seemed to devote itself entirely to a life of relaxation and enjoyment. The open-air cafés were full of activity and carefree business, while the promenade was a fashionable rendezvous for the smartly-dressed people.

On the way home from Nictheroy we passed a harbour steamer, whose obvious mission sent a cold shudder down our backs. It was none other than the ambulance boat well known to every sailor who had been to Rio, and was dubbed by them the "dead" boat. It made periodic trips round the harbour and collected sick and fatal cases from ships. When a vessel required medical aid, the national flag was flown on the fore, and much excitement and morbid curiosity was evinced by all the other ships. Binoculars would be busy watching the unfortunate stricken one being lowered over the side, whilst a small parcel of clothing would be hurled through the air after him.

We had occasion to fly the flag once, and that was to remove Erick, but he had looked as though ready to go at any time. Although an excellent sailor, he was a most delicate man. His place was taken before we sailed by a recovery case, who had been left behind by his ship—a cockney named Pane—and he turned out to be a great acquisition. Pane was gifted with a true cockney wit that was equal at any time to a draught of champagne. To listen to him recounting his experiences in the hospital during his period of convalescence was most entertaining. Apparently the hospital staff were anxious to learn English, and what Billy Pane taught them, one shuddered to think. His vocabulary was limited but forceful.

One day I went ashore with the Captain. And in order to keep me occupied while he transacted the ship's business, he told me to find out, if I could, where a certain cemetery was in which a young sailor from Portmadoc, who had died at Rio some years previously, had been buried.

My task was not an easy one. Having climbed a good distance in what I was told was the right direction, I met two Portuguese coming out of the gate of a large institution. I went over to them to make further inquiries, and to my horror, they turned out to be discharged smallpox cases, leaving the hospital. Their faces resembled plum puddings with the currants much in evidence. I do not know what they thought of me, for having discovered from about five yards' distance what they were, I turned tail, and ran away terrified.

Badly shaken, but undismayed in my desire to carry out the mission, I decided to try my luck by calling at a house close by. There I succeeded in rallying a large family, who by their interest might have been useful had they been able to understand English. They led me to a neighbour's house, where one of the sons, who had recently returned from Europe, was supposed to have studied English. However, with the aid of a Portuguese-English and an English-Portuguese dictionary, we got on excellently, so much so, that we succeeded in bringing both families to a keen pitch of excitement. It was much like piecing together a puzzle, with the answer becoming vaguely apparent when halfway through.

Having refreshed ourselves with (from my point of view) a most delicious cup of coffee (real Brazil coffee), I was taken in a horse-drawn carriage of the "buggy" variety through very beautiful grounds to the cemetery. We walked through a tremendous burial ground accompanied by an attendant, and discovered that the part of the cemetery that we wanted had recently been turned over for reburial purposes, and we were shown another part in course of undergoing similar treatment. Ends of coffins could be seen jutting out of the soil, and the sight was sickening. There was no sign of the grave of the Welsh sailor from Portmadoc. I was glad when I regained the peaceful precincts of the ship, for I was rather upset by the gruesome experience.

5

HUMMING BIRDS

We were told on no account to leave Rio until we had seen the famous view from the top of the Corcovado. I was not very enthusiastic. The fear of smallpox and a general sense of depression hung

heavily on me. I felt safer and happier on board
the *Pride of Wales*. In the Captain's case it did
not matter much, as he had only recently recovered
from a severe attack of smallpox which he con-
tracted at Santos, a place close by; so his will
prevailed, and we set off at an early hour in order
to benefit by the cooler part of the day.

It was a wonderful trip, and I must admit I
would not have missed the experience for anything. It turned out to be one of those memorable
days in one's career, filled with wonders of a new
and novel kind.

With really very little fatigue, we reached a point
well above the built-up part of the town, and
finding a snug recess sheltered from the distressing
rays of the sun, we rested under palm trees. We
lunched on local wine and sandwiches from the
ship. All around us was a riot of wild flowers
and a confusion of tropical vegetation.

And humming birds came to entertain us. These
humming birds were the first I had seen enjoying
to the full the freedom of native surroundings. It
is uncanny how they can hover in mid-air in front
of a flower and remain in what appears to be a
stationary position, purely by wing manipulation,
and the wings vibrate so rapidly that they seem
to be not moving at all. The humming birds
approach so closely to the petals that they are
able to thrust their abnormally long black beaks
into the heart of the flower, where they expect to
find a tasty morsel. Rapidly changing position and
direction, they are off to the next flower, and it
is at this instant that the hum from which they
derive their name is heard more distinctly, and
so their diligent search for food continues amid

the most pleasant surroundings and a plethora of bloom.

The radiant and rich colour of their plumage is seen to the best advantage when their hunger is satisfied and they are perched on twigs titivating their feathers. Each turn of the head reveals ever-changing shades of green, blending into a ruby-red throat, which, in some species, is adorned also with an Elizabethan kind of neck frill. But I think the chief charm of the humming birds lies in their diminutive size. They are much smaller than our smallest wren, and being so richly coloured they look more like an animated trinket than members of the feathered world. Like most small things, they have an overabundance of self-assurance and lose no opportunity in asserting themselves. They seem always ready to dart pugnaciously at birds much larger than themselves, and apparently get away with it, for the larger birds flee in fear. The humming birds refuse to be tamed into cage birds. They have probably made up their minds that if they cannot enjoy their freedom and their very specially-selected diet, they would rather die.

Butterflies, too, fluttered into the scene, as if turned out of an artist's studio close by. They seemed jealous of the admiration extended to the wild flowers, the humming birds and the parra-keets, and as we sat there, as quiet as mice, much engrossed in this pageantry, we subconsciously felt that we had been specially invited into this sanctum to give an impartial opinion in this keen competition of things beautiful.

The butterfly is a specialist in the art of dis-playing his lovely vestments, for he is neither timid nor in any great hurry to pass by. They would follow each other to the same flower in a resplendent procession. Here they would remain with palpitating outstretched wings, long enough to impress us with their particular pattern of design and tint schemes. They exhibited almost every conceivable shade of blue, ranging from a delicate French grey to a dark peacock, glistening with a metallic lustre, and an infinite variety of species, some small and brooch-like, others as large as one's hand; but whether large or small, they were each equally beautiful. No wonder that to many a keen scientist Brazil is best known as the land of butterflies.

6

MONKEYS AND PARROTS

After lunch and the humming birds and the butterflies we climbed higher to get an uninterrupted view of what must rank surely as one of the most majestic sights in the whole world.

Beneath us lay a great city, populated by a million souls made up of many races and types of humanity, but perhaps with the Portuguese predominant. One would naturally expect to find Nature's work, however beautiful, ruined by the variety of accommodation needed to house such numbers. But such is not the case with Rio. Man's work, in this instance, seems to have added to, rather than detracted from, the charms of the place. This is accounted for in two ways. First of all because of the contour and the well-wooded nature of the ridges which run from the Carioca range, skirting the quaint Hunch Mountain on their way down to the clear water of the bay.

Upon these ridges, the city is built in artistic terraces. The large houses and institutions have spacious grounds and well-stocked gardens. There is never a dearth of flowers and luxuriant tropical trees.

Not only does each building face the majestic bay and hinterland, but it has also its own immediate view over luxuriant valleys to the neighbouring spurs on either side. Secondly, owing to the place enjoying perpetual summer weather, the inhabitants are able to dispense with our usual fires and ugly chimney stacks. Fogs are almost unknown, so that all the buildings which are painted white or a lightish colour contrast pleasingly with the green, grey, and blue surroundings. As the many spurs vary in the distance they penetrate into the bay, so in turn this gives the city the many gracefully-curved promenades which I saw in full illumination from the cross trees on the night of our arrival.

On the extreme right is situated the most beautiful of the bays, known as Botofago. It stretches from the Sugar Loaf mountain in the shape of a horse-shoe. This bay has a marble promenade, and no expense has been spared to make it one of the handsomest sea fronts in the world.

Turning slightly in the direction of the sea, the coastal mountain range outside the harbour could be followed in both directions. The awesome irregularity of the towering heights, broken at frequent intervals by silvery bathing strands, is perpetually washed by the breakers of the Atlantic. Each bay is attractively laid out as a seaside resort, and all the bays are much frequented on account of their nearness to the city.

Another of Rio's charms is to be found in the absence of hideous dockland. Possessing as it does great natural resources as a harbour and being free from tidal influences, all the ships lie at anchor, dotted all over the bay. The aristocrats of the sea, the large wind-jammers, are given a central position, midway between Rio and Nictheroy. Here they disport themselves, showing the full charm of their elegance in an ideal colouring and setting. So large is the bay that it would hold at the same time all the navies of the world without one ship jostling another. Quite close to the wind-jammers, a roadstead was allocated to ships of war of all nations, and next to them were passenger steamers and mail boats. On the left of the harbour were congregated all the small coastal sailing vessels, mostly flying Portuguese, Spanish, and South American State flags. All these ships, almost without exception, were painted white, giving that portion of the anchorage a touch reminiscent of the Solent in the month of August.

Girdling the entire bay, some distance away, was the great range of the Organ Mountains, rising to the height of seven thousand feet. The slopes —a wooded wilderness—are untouched by the hand of man. The fantastic shapes of the peaks gave them an appearance of uncommon grandeur. Not far away stood the rock formations known as the Five Fingers of God. These elongated granite peaks resembling monstrous fingers, are surely aptly named; and Rio indeed stands out as a masterpiece of God's work. On the summit of the quaintly-shaped Corcovado is now erected a statue of Christ, with outstretched arms. It is flood-lit, and, being two thousand feet high, it can be seen far out at sea. The sight must be most impressive.

We watched the departure for sea of H.M.S. *Cleopatra*, a small barque-rigged British warship which was the Flagship of the South American station. We could but notice how diminutive she looked as she passed quite close to the large four-masted full-rigged ship *Afghanistan*, which was empty. Following in the *Cleopatra's* wake came an American coffee clipper, a two-thousand-ton four-masted fore-and-aft-rigged sailing vessel, running between Rio and the Northern States of America, carrying the world's most delicious coffee to the American people. They were lovely ships, and quite different from our idea of clippers—four tall masts, scraped and sun-bleached, looking much like ivory. On these were set but twelve sails made of perfect material known as American Cotton Canvas, and fitting faultlessly. Their spars and sails were the envy of the world. Black hulls, white deck-fittings and high bows gave them a business-like appearance; and they could sail.

The ship's complement was much augmented by the time we were ready to leave Rio. Monkeys, marmosets, parrots, and parrakeets squeaked and chattered all over the deck. These additions certainly created a new and novel atmosphere which was quite in keeping with the order of things as long as we remained in the tropics, but sadly out of place when we got into the wintry conditions of the North Atlantic, where many funerals had to be organised.

Olaf had exchanged odds and ends of much-used clothes for a marmoset, and was much pleased with his bargain. He had added a specially-made breast pocket to most of his shirts and jumpers, and here the little fellow loved to be. It was most amusing to see his pretty and fascinating face full of a curious expression peeping out between a centre button of the pocket and the edge, appearing to take a keen interest in all that went on, whether Olaf was high up in the rigging at work or sitting yarning on the fo'c'sle head during hours of leisure. If a spray caught him in the face he would appear to sneeze and would then rub his eyes with the back of his hand in a very human manner, and eventually withdraw out of sight until more pleasant conditions prevailed.

The presence of so many pets gave much displeasure to one man, the boatswain. They made him bristle more than ever; not that he particularly disliked birds and beasts in their proper environment, but he could not reconcile such an artificial atmosphere with the hard-going of a wind-jammer. He was an old-fashioned type of sailor that looked upon the life as a very serious business, and the thought of turning the ship into a sort of menagerie was repugnant in the extreme. He frequently expressed the view that there were quite enough oddities on board before the arrival of the monkeys and parrots.

He must have thoroughly enjoyed a joke the Captain played on me the day we left Rio. We weighed anchor soon after dawn and breakfast was to be taken when we had cleared port. It happened that my favourite breakfast was "on" that morning. I had recognised the full aroma of a highly-seasoned hash (which was the cook's masterpiece) as we rushed about the decks busily setting sails. It was only necessary to gain the open sea to realise that none of that pie would be mine after all, for an exceptionally brisk breeze and a choppy sea soon counted me out. Sea-sickness had once again claimed me a victim. Curling down in one of the boats on the skids, I cared not who had the pie. Regaining consciousness a little later in the day, I was amused to find that the Captain had placed in the boat with me my two sea-sick parrots and a monkey who was also very sorry for himself. On the thwarts he had pinned this notice: "DRAWING-ROOM SAILORS FOR SALE" and "SURRENDER OF THE CHATTERBOXES."

I ought to say that owing to watch arrangements I seldom had occasion to come in contact with the boatswain at sea, but he found my volubility in port most irritating to his nature. I was glad I was not posted to his watch, for Hans, who was boiling over with the joy of youth, was continually stalked by his relentless discipline. On the slightest suspicion of effervescence he would be handed a grease spot and sent aloft for long duration to grease down. This was a job that stilled one's *joie de vivre* effectively. How one longed for some sort of revenge! Sometimes when at the wheel a sly luff of a point or two would cause a lump of sea to be shipped somewhere in the region of the enemy and give him annoyance and the perpetrator much joy; but the joy had to be of the silent and expressionless variety, which robbed the occasion of a deal of its pleasure.

CHAPTER V

Sharks

I

DOG OVERBOARD

THE great Organ Mountains had at last vanished beyond the distant horizon. It was pleasing to see the purple glow of the setting sun again. We were on the high seas and heading for the "Line."

A refreshing and cooling breeze fanned our faces. Five weeks at oppressive Rio had brought about much languor and debility among us. A sailor's lot in a tropical port is not altogether a happy one. Discharging cargo becomes one of his many duties, and the work is fatiguing, heavy, and monotonous. The food was invariably ill-chosen for the climate, with the result that vitality was always on the ebb. The constant fear of illness, too, played on the mind and racked the nerves.

This was my first experience of the *Pride of Wales* in ballast trim, and I found it both novel and pleasant. To begin with, we were out of reach of sea and spray, and the old ship was bouncing over the waves like a large rubber toy. With every sail set she heeled over steeply to the boisterous breeze of the south-east trade. We were bound for a small island called Aruba in the Dutch Antilles, four thousand miles away. I will later explain

why we sailed this great distance to pick up a
cargo.

The passage was filled with exciting incidents
and things of interest. On the dawn of the second
day we found a small sailing ship quite close under
our bows. Both ships were steering the same
course, and we were slowly catching her up. We
had always considered the *Pride of Wales* to be
one of the smallest barques afloat, but here was
one much smaller. She was of Portuguese
nationality, and very pretty to look at. The
impression was that she had at one time been a
yacht and had fallen on evil days—finishing up a
gay life humping merchandise across the sea. She
was loaded deep down, and with such graceful
lines looked odd and out of place. She, too, with
twenty-two sails set, revelled in the breeze and
jumped at the billows with much abandon. I
believe, given level terms, she would have shown
us a clean pair of heels. A large dog of the Labrador
retriever variety raced about her deck and seemed
to take a most human interest in our presence and
in the general proceedings. When both ships were
quite close together he took up a challenging
attitude with front paws on the taffrail—how dare
any ship pass his! He barked furiously and
became very excited, so much so that he fell overboard. There were but three men visible on the
little ship's deck at the time; nevertheless she was
brought rattling into the wind in an instant, coming
uncomfortably close to us in so doing. Two men
hurled a scow (a small boat) into the sea; they
jumped over the side and swam to it.

It was soon apparent that the rescue work under-
taken by these two brave and compassionate sea-

men was going to be difficult and perilous. The sea on this occasion was much too boisterous for a small flimsily-constructed boat to live in. We watched the little cockle shell, and its two occupants, with breathless excitement. It could be seen bobbing up and down, splashing and battling its way heroically towards the unfortunate dog. The dog's sagacity was not amiss either. He could be seen through the binoculars keeping a dead straight course for the little boat and swimming with all the pluck imaginable. He might have been out doing his daily dozen. Within a few minutes the dog, the seamen, and the tiny boat were all safely on board again. Both ships proceeded on their course.

Sailors become sentimentally attached to ships' pets, and this sort of thing is of quite common occurrence.

A week later we were rolling drowsily a few degrees south of the Equator. A white kitten belonging to the cabin was jumping playfully up and down the poop deck. The Captain and I were much entertained by its frolics. Suddenly it sprang in the wrong direction, which was overboard. We were at that time sailing through shark-infested waters, and wondered what the kitten's fate would be. A seaman proceeding to steering duties seeing what had happened instantly leapt into the sea, and swimming strongly, succeeded in reaching the terrified kitten. Fortunately we were nearly becalmed at the time, and the seaman was able to regain the ship's side. So tightly had he gripped the poor beast, that it was nearly dead from strangulation.

It may be asked—What about the sharks? Well,

sharks are the most timid of creatures, and so long as there is plenty of splashing going on, the shark will keep his distance. It is when the struggle is weakening that he gets busy, and lays hold.

The Dutch Antilles is a group of small, low, rocky and barren islands. They are dotted close together in the track of the north-east trade wind off the coast of Venezuela. Why such bleak places should exist in such a delightful climate is difficult to understand. The most important is Curaçao, with Aruba on its western side, and Buen Ayre on the eastern. Another little lump called Little Curaçao nestles close to the parent isle. In order to add to their unromantic appearance and character—and it seemed to make them more secure against the intrusion of man—they are guarded by a dangerous system of coral reefs.

Looking at them cursorily, one would form the opinion that they were admirably appointed and adapted for what Nature had meant them to be—a sanctuary for an innumerable variety of sea birds and a home for countless fish. The stunted growth of the few trees that could be seen gave the islands a sinister appearance, each contorted tree bending its head wearily towards the setting sun, testifying that all hope had been given up of the wind ever changing from E. This blissful immunity from the interference of man that the birds had enjoyed through unknown centuries was not to continue for aye.

One day, the chattering multitude became much alarmed. They saw appearing from the sea the inquisitive hand of Science. It climbed their rugged foreshore and probed stealthily in their midst. It descended their sacred chasms and crevices and dug deep into their homes. Here was found under the rocky surface, hidden away in great stratas, a mineral of much commercial value, known as Phosphate of Lime. So these Ugly Ducklings of the Caribbean soon became most valuable assets to the Dutch Exchequer.

Great quarries were set in motion. Loud explosions of rock blasted by dynamite and the puffing of engines drove many of the birds to look for more peaceful surroundings to rear their young.

Without delving too deeply into chemistry, I will briefly explain how Nature manufactured on a very large scale this much-sought-after and valuable mineral.

Guano is the all-important constituent necessary for its manufacture, and owing to the uninterrupted occupation of the islands by birds, there was no dearth of this. During the wet season, torrential rain percolated through the guano and in so doing dissolved the rich acid phosphates contained therein. The phosphates were thus carried by the escaping floods into a limestone stratum under the surface. Here chemical reaction took place. The acid phosphates of the guano and the alkaline of the limestone united and formed the staple compound Phosphate of Calcium, commercially known as phosphate rock.

It exists as a heavy quartz, so heavy that a wooden vessel literally groaned under the burden when loaded with it. Aruba alone up to 1870 had shipped half a million tons. So the magnitude of this simple process of Nature can be realised.

2

HAZARDOUS TRADE

Owing to primitive harbour facilities, the task of conveying phosphate rock across the Atlantic had to be entrusted entirely to small sailing ships. It was considered to be one of the most hazardous trades that any vessel could be engaged in. The toll of failures was abnormally high. The bed of the ocean from the Dutch Antilles to the Channel is studded with the corpses of ships and sailors that had failed to accomplish the strenuous undertaking.

There was a great demand in England and Northern Europe for this rich mineral, and in order to induce little ships to take on the risky work, attractive rates were paid for its transportation.

I have now come to the reason why we were sailing four thousand miles in ballast. The phosphate carrier got the big shilling.

Our skipper had been to Aruba three times previously, but only once with the *Pride of Wales*. He used to say that he had been lucky to reach the other side of the Atlantic on each occasion. The thought of a recurrence of those experiences now haunted him. He had a prescience that the next would ring the death knell of all concerned. It appeared, too, that his confidence in the *Pride of Wales*, now on the venerable side, was waning. He could sense her chances of fighting through diminishing. He knew the mood in which we should find the North Atlantic during the months of October and November. His mind was filled with anxieties. I must say that, during such ideal weather conditions through which we were passing then, I found it difficult to absorb even a small measure of these gloomy possibilities. But experienced mariners do all their hard thinking and worrying in fine weather. It is their "prep" time. When difficult days come, they adapt themselves to the conditions subconsciously. When the storm rages they seem to be in their rightful atmosphere.

The old "hulk," which she had been called many a time when little bits of equipment carried away in fine weather, suddenly became a "grand little lady" and a "good old gal" when she parried the monster wave and fought the tempest to a standstill. On those occasions all doubts are dispelled. It is a time when courage holds the sway and much faith prevails.

I remember on one occasion when, at the peak of a great storm, a man broke away from his job and, kneeling, began to pray. Presently a powerful sea boot sent him on his way with the remark, "This is not a fit day for missionaries to be out. Get a move on, sonny!"

3

A DREAM ISLAND

There was one thing that young sailors, particularly, found very difficult to do on board ship, and that was to keep awake during the night watches. I suffered many punishments from an insistent desire to sleep after midnight. If it was a turn at the wheel or look-out duties, the feared consequences were usually sufficient to ward off sleep; but "farmer duties," as they were known,

which meant just waiting for something to turn
up in the form of a command, were most trying.
One loitered about the deck and gazed vacantly
into the darkness. I frequently found myself
collapsing slowly on such occasions.

Once I had gone to sleep in this way, and I
was discovered. I was immediately sent up aloft
to do a job of work. My imposition was to stop
(tie up) on the jackstays, bunt lines and leech lines
on every one of the ten yards. These ropes, prior
to my slumber, were quite secure, but in order to
give punishment and also make sure that it would
keep me awake, the necessity of sending me aloft
had been created. It was done by jerking these
ropes adrift with a sharp tug, which could be performed from the deck. It was an old trick. If it
was thought that I was being punished by being
sent aloft, it was a mistake, for I had arrived at
the stage of thoroughly enjoying skipping in the
rigging and balancing myself on my diaphragm on
a rocking spar.

I have heard many people say how majestic and
beautiful a sailing vessel looked when passing by
under full sail. I quite agree; but more beautiful
still is she when seen from high up her own masts,
her white sails tightly stretched across the skies,
each straining at the leash to gather a share of
life and power from the freshening breeze. When
I got up to the fore top gallant yard, having finished
the main mast in the light of the stars, I witnessed
a gorgeous sunrise, worth all the punishment in
the world. A silver rim of the rising sun peeped
coyly over the horizon. It seemed almost to
apologise for disturbing the delicious cool air of the
night. Soon it was framed in bars of golden cloud.

The entire eastern sky was of delicate jade green, a most unusual effect. To the left of the sun I could see a perfect outline of a small island, a very long way away. The island stood out so clearly on the horizon that it was unmistakable, and although it vanished within a few minutes like a dream, it remained long enough to impress me with its strange outline. It had two or three sharp peaks, and one much like the shape of the Sugar Loaf at Rio. Where could it be?

When I returned on deck I reported it in the usual way, and gave a bearing, but it did not seem to interest any one very much. But at breakfast, the Captain took it up, and when working out the ship's position he told me that I had seen Fernando Noronah, a lonely island a hundred and twenty miles from the Brazilian coast. It is used as a convict settlement by the State of Brazil. I could make the proud boast that I was the only one in the ship who had seen Fernando Noronah.

We later sighted a coraline group of rocks, just showing their sharp teeth above the sea. Terrible things in any other part of the world, except perhaps in a similar place to this, they nevertheless seemed very popular with sea birds; and the area was alive with fish, but we were travelling too fast to catch any.

4

THE AMAZON

We were now sailing parallel with the north coast of South America, along the torrid zone. Running dead before the wind and covering about

a hundred and eighty miles a day, we had struck
an extremely hot patch. The main deck was so
hot that shoes had to be worn to get about during
the day. The pitch that filled the deck seams
bubbled, and the clean decks soon became thoroughly messy.

Sailing east to west, with the sun rapidly
approaching the directly overhead position at noon,
and the wind dead aft, is most trying. Sleep during
the day was out of the question, and the few
square sails set offered little shade.

One morning there was great excitement when
the man at the wheel shouted "Breakers ahead!"
There was a feverish scramble to get on deck from
the breakfast table. The Captain said it was non-
sense, but when he had reached the fore-top he
changed his mind. The horizon ahead from north
to south was a seething mass of broken water,
more accentuated this day because the wind had
dropped considerably and we were more or less in
smooth conditions. Shoals or rocks could be ruled
out quickly, for the nearest land on the course
that we were steering was many hundred of miles
away.

"A tidal wave" flashed through the minds of
most of us, but the Captain, on referring to his
chart, soon reassured us; we were approaching the
eastern edge of the efflux of the river Amazon.

This great river, four thousand miles in length,
was a law unto itself. Even at this extraordinary
distance of two hundred miles out at sea it was
still forcing its way with great turbulence and
determination against the more peaceful equatorial
current that was moving at right angles to it.
What an awesome moment, when we plunged from

the rich blue of the ocean to this yellow-coloured turmoil! It took us the best part of two days to sail through until we reached the other edge. The Captain computed the breadth to be within the region of two hundred and fifty miles. It turned out to be quite an interesting event; and another page of sea life was written that day.

5

SHARK FISHING

We discovered very quickly that the area was infested with sharks. They forgather there in order to enjoy the refuse and sweepings of thousands of miles of the muddy, insanitary, and notoriously unhealthy banks of the second largest river in the world. What a happy hunting ground for the sea's greatest scavenger, and what an excellent mood we found him in! True to his rapacious nature and game to the last gasp. Every sailor knows what a horribly one-sided and short-lived contest it was, and, how ruthless and bloody, when shark and sailor met on the former's territory. But believe me, it is just as bad when the position is reversed and the sailor has the upper hand and the venue is the deck of a ship.

A sailor is quite a rational thinking man in the ordinary way, and will risk his life freely for the service, but mention the word "shark" and he boils over in a minute. He shudders actually at the thought of that progressive amputation which the shark practises. To the sailor, the sea would be rid of half its terrors if all the sharks were caught and slaughtered.

On that day we accounted for three of the brutes. We were moving along at about four knots in a smoothish stream. Close under the ship's counter, we could see under the surface, darting to and fro in an excited manner, a small fish much like a mackerel but with yellow stripes. He is known as the pilot fish, and is always attached to the H.Q. staff of the shark.

It has puzzled the experts why this dapper little fellow should associate himself so completely with this master, this ugly omnivorous terror. He never seems to share in his ill-gotten gains, and yet his loyalty is constant and profound. He takes up his position a few yards in front and above, and is constantly returning to his master's side with signals of any danger that may be near and news of any tit-bit that he thinks will delight and appease his master's voracious appetite.

And why does a shark need a scout? One would imagine the shark quite capable of finding his own meals. He is exceedingly active and has a most efficient jaw, both in size and quality, and teeth to deal with almost anything that swims. Nor is it that he is particular or fussy in his diet and requires someone as a taster, for he will eat any rubbish, anything, dead or alive, fresh or stale, and he never seems to have had enough.

One of the three we caught with a five-pound bait of fat pork had a recently-devoured dolphin snugly packed inside. This is quite unusual, as the dolphin is much faster than a shark. What must have happened was that the dolphin was probably having a look round the ship's hull with his accustomed inquisitiveness, and was evidently caught unawares.

The entire crew were desirous of joining in the fun of catching sharks. The fishing (slaughter) party was under the command of Old Bristly, and not only was he a real leader but he could deal most ably with every phase of the operations. Bristly would never smoke when on a stunt, but would revert to the chewing habit, and lustily did he chew. From each corner of his mouth deep wrinkles ran down his chin, almost surrounding it. They were known to the sailor as "pea-soup channels." One could always tell Mondays and Wednesdays, which were pea-soup days, by looking at Bristly's face, for on those days there was ample evidence in the channels. But on this occasion they were the channels for tobacco juice.

The boatswain considered shark-killing a real sailor's job. He could sense a day of good hunting, and soon became keyed up to a high pitch of excitement and enthusiasm. Stripped to the waist, his face covered with a growth of coarse and stumpy beard, his long grey wiry hair standing erect, he looked terrible enough for any deed. A parrot in a cage swaying under the mizzen boom gazed at him suspiciously through one eye and chattered, but Bristly was in no mood to talk to parrots, being deeply preoccupied burying a rusty shark hook in a chunk of fat pork.

Leaning over the ship's side to spit copiously of the juice of tobacco, he saw a vicious beast turning and twisting swiftly below. Mustering his party, he jumped out on the bumpkin in order to dangle the bait clear of the ship's side. With Bristly in this dangerous position, the shark must have had an excellent and appetising view of a large expanse of white human flesh for which he must have longed. He leapt wildly into the air. "*All right*," said the boatswain. "*You vait, you zon of a beetch, ve voss zoon ready for you. . . .*"

The equipment necessary to deal with a shark consisted of a half-inch wrought-iron hook a foot long, with a yard of chain attached and a good stout rope for a line. As the bait and hook usually disappear well down the shark's gullet, it is necessary to have this yard of chain on the line in order to give him something to sharpen his teeth on. At the end of the line, four stout seamen were necessary even with a moderate-sized fish, say five or six feet in length, and I have seen the perspiration rolling off their faces after twenty minutes' play.

Half-way through the afternoon we angled for a big one, but it took a considerable time before he could be persuaded to do what his brothers had done earlier on. He was recommended by his aide-de-camp, the pilot fish, on several occasions to partake of the feast prepared for him, and once or twice he came up from the depths at a great pace, the white flash of his underside being plainly visible as he rolled over in readiness to attack. But after taking a quick look at the now very bleached pork, he made a sharp turn, slashed the surface of the sea with his powerful tail in disgust, and darted out of sight. He did not quite fancy that particular piece. Whether he could detect that the bait had been used for the other two or not, we did not know. However, we got him later with a change of bait—a bloody portion of the flesh of his own tribe was used. It was first of all quickly dipped in the sea and drawn up again, leaving a pool of gore on the surface. This the pilot fish thoroughly recommended. We then slowly lowered the real bait towards the sea. Without any more to do, up came the shark from a great depth at a terrific speed, leapt three feet into the air, and swallowed the lot. He looked quite ten feet long. Instantly he seemed to know that he had been fooled, for he jumped about the surface of the sea in a state of maddened fury trying to get rid of the hook. When the fishing party administered the first check, he plunged perpendicularly downwards, and took the whole length of the line. But the rope was a good one, and his fate was sealed. It took five men half an hour to get him to the ship's side for the first time. And what exciting sport it was. We eventually got him on the boat davits. Whilst in this position he lashed the ship's side furiously with his tail, his open mouth showing rows of vicious teeth. The chain, which in the morning was rusty, was now burnished like silver. A determined effort was made to subdue his rage and to wheedle him into a mood of good behaviour and composure, which was very necessary if he was to come on board. We in due course swung him inboard for the final rites. Johann, a Swedish A.B. who claimed to be the most recent one on board to have lost a relative at sea, was given the honour of administering the *coup de grâce*. He was ceremoniously presented with a capstan bar, and was requested to sever the vertebra, two feet above the tail. While Johann was at the top of his swing the old shark seemed to know what was about to happen, for he threw his final convulsion and leapt about the deck wildly; this made Johann

miss the mark altogether, but he managed to slay
one of the ship's cats which had come up on deck
for the kill. Strangely enough, this particular old
cat never came on deck unless there was fish about.
He had beaten me many a night in the race for
flying fish. On this occasion, he rushed in between
our legs for a tit-bit, but was just unlucky and
caught Johann's full swing.

Later on in the dim light of a globe lamp the
boatswain and his entourage filed out to the end
of the jib-boom, where the tail of the big shark
was nailed, as a symbol of revenge and a warning
to others.

6

FLOATING ISLAND

That night at a ghoulish hour I was yarning with
Pane as we paced the for'ard-deck, keeping the
lookout. In the galley close by flickered a fire. On
the stove was a large dixie which contained the
head of one of the sharks. It was being boiled
to separate the flesh from the jaw. A strong odour
came in wafts to disturb our pleasure, but from
my point of view it was worth tolerating, for I
was to possess a perfect specimen of a shark's jaw
to commemorate the epic day. Suddenly between
the clew of the fore-sail and the red glow of the
navigation light we saw a strange sight which for
a moment made us stand aghast. What looked
like a hideous monster was rapidly approaching
through the darkness. Its great body heaved on
the billows. So grim and uncanny was the atmosphere that for the moment we were terrified. Were
the slaughtered sharks to be avenged by some

greater demon of the deep? The ship suddenly changed course. The din of flapping sails and the shrill voice of the Chief ordering the yards to be trimmed increased the excitement.

The Captain, awakened by the running braces, was soon on deck. Focusing the object with his binoculars, he recognised one of the great river's eccentricities. A huge floating island was swooping into the ocean. Litter and garbage of the eight thousand miles of banks and shores of the Amazon and its tributaries, consisting of trees and branches, feathery grasses, huge leaves, chunks of wood, packing mats, disused fruit baskets, bamboos, carcases of beasts, old clothing and what not collect and knit together to form these roving islands. Frequently trees and tropical vegetation grow and thrive on them. These self-made islands do not last long in the open sea, where a storm soon disintegrates them.

We were now making for the small Dutch island called Buen Ayre. There was something about this part of the passage quite different from what we had experienced during the four thousand miles' run from Rio. A more perfect climate it is difficult to imagine. There was glorious sunshine the whole day long. It was not too hot, and there was an exhilarating breeze varying little in its velocity. There was a brightness and lightness about everything that was a tonic for the body and the soul. Although the sea was a thousand fathoms deep, it was a totally different colour from that of the ocean; a delightful greenish hue surrounded us.

We had a thrilling experience off Buen Ayre. It is an odd story. In the February of that same year, a small barque, owned in Portmadoc, called

Coconut Plantation, Trinidad

FACE PAGE 97

Lone palm, the only tree on the lowlands of
Ascension Island

the *Cuerero*, was bound from a South Atlantic port for Aruba. When off Buen Ayre she struck a coral reef in broad daylight, and sank in a few minutes, without leaving a trace of visible wreckage, and that was the end of her. Running our south-westerly course, quite close to the island, the Captain was explaining to me what had happened to the *Cuerero*, and that in his opinion it was one of those cases which were difficult to explain away. Approaching the most southerly point of the island, we expected to find a lighthouse, which was shown on the chart to exist, indicating the extent and direction of a reef, but with the exception of one or two white huts or cottages there was nothing on the headland looking anything like a lighthouse that sailors are accustomed to. We were sailing gaily with every sail set. The trade wind was brisk that day and was on the port quarters. The sun had about two hours to go before setting, and was dead ahead, throwing a blinding glare on the entire sea and horizon. The Captain and I were sitting on a seat on the cabin skylight, chatting happily, and looking at the rough contour of the little island as it flashed by our beam. We were reeling off ten knots. The light-house had been forgotten and we imagined that we were far enough off land to clear any reef.

Olaf, who was at the wheel, suddenly sang out: "Breakers ahead, sir, and there is the lighthouse, four points on the weather bow." We had been talking such a lot about this lighthouse, that for the moment the Captain thought Olaf was mis-taken. But one glance to windward disclosed a large lighthouse dancing in the silvery glare, almost like a ghost pointing to our doom.

G

Angry-looking breakers, caused by the equatorial current crashing against the reef, were whipped ten feet into the air, and they extended as far as the eye could follow towards the shore. We were sailing at full speed for the centre of the reef where the *Cuerero* foundered, and it looked as if we would take our place beside her in less than a twinkling. The next few minutes were most exciting and thrilling. It was a wonderful sight to see this little vessel on her mettle, settling down to extricate herself from the jaws of death, heeling over to a dangerous angle, struggling under a terrific burden of canvas, for when close hauled we realised how hard it was blowing. Would she gain the open sea?

As far as it was possible to judge, the farther we went the nearer we seemed to get to the reef. The Captain took up his position at the wheel, directing Olaf how to steal every possible inch to windward, yet without lifting a leech to check her speed. Orders were given to swing the life-boat out on the davits and prepare to take in royals, top-gallant sails and mainsail. Were these orders the prelude to disaster? No! the former was merely precautionary, and the latter a masterly stroke of seamanship, which was put into effect when all seemed over. By keeping only the fore and aft sails and the four top sails set, at the critical moment it was possible to gain at least ten degrees to windward, which now brought the lighthouse well under our lee. In an instant it could be seen we were clear, but only with a couple of ship's lengths to spare. Phew!

The glare caused by the afternoon sun setting on our course was responsible for the danger. Had it been morning or night, all would have been well.

More islands loomed up ahead before nightfall, little Curaçao and the larger one. From there the famous liqueur takes its name. We could have done with a tot that night to celebrate our escape, but apparently all the island does towards producing the nectar is to grow a peculiar orange, the peel of which alone is required. This is shipped to Europe, where the liqueur is manufactured.

7

DESOLATE ISLE

We hung under the lee of Curaçao all that night, as Aruba can only be negotiated by a sailing ship in light trim, in daylight. There must exist a perfect understanding between ship and shore. Should a vessel be at the entrance before a pilot boat is outside, actually waiting, then the sailing ship slips by and her chance is lost. Nothing more can be done until she has made a detour of many hundreds of miles and makes a second attempt, remembering the expensive lesson taught by the previous occasion.

Our pilot was a one-armed man, but he had a vicious substitute for the other—a sharp hook which he dug into everything. He ruined our steering wheel which was a much-prized polished fitting. He was known to terrify natives with it, too.

Everything, however, went in our favour; and at noon we had anchored in this tiny harbour of Fort Zoutman. What a place! My goodness!

What a place! In ten fleeting minutes we seemed
to have slipped back to a prehistoric age. Alongside of a home-made wharf lay a small West-
Country schooner, the only ship in the place. A
real little clipper, so small that one felt sorry to
see her so far from her Cornish home, and covered
from deck to truck with a grey dust. She had just
finished loading this phosphatised limestone, the
island's only produce of note in those days. The
rock was conveyed from quarries in the heart of
the island down to the quay by a narrow-gauge
railway, very roughly laid. The trucks were hauled
by a small engine, which was full of importance
when it whistled, for it usually meant that it and
the trucks had left the metals somewhere. When
we arrived, it whistled us a hearty welcome. I
think the driver remembered the *Pride of Wales*
from her previous visits. He was probably drawing
the Captain's attention to the fact that he could do
with a drink.

The harbour seemed to have been taken over
by pelicans and other strange sea birds. They
revelled in the abundance of fish that the harbour
held. I was intrigued by the pelican's habits and
his unique way of filling his larder (his beak). It
was exciting to watch him hurl his huge dishevelled
form from a height of about a hundred feet, hitting the sea a terrific crash with his clumsy body
—much like a bag of flour falling from the skies;
but he never failed to secure a choice fish. Like
the shark, his appetite seems to be beyond
satisfying.

Fishing from the jollyboat, I was much annoyed
to see a native urchin amusing himself by killing
these interesting birds in a most cruel and in-

human manner. He swam out from an adjacent beach and placed a flat board on the surface of the water. On the board was nailed a fish, probably a pet one of the pelican's. The boy would then swim inshore and watch events from behind a boulder. The bird, seeing this easy prey, would do his usual swoop, only to crash and break his neck on the hard board. Filled with anger, I made for the beach to remonstrate with the offender, but I found that he could deal with me as easily as he could with the pelican. I came away with a swollen lip and a black eye.

One would expect better things from a place bearing such a name as Fort Zoutman. There was not even an interesting allusion to either name. There was no town, not even a village. No streets, no shops, no pavements, no roads, no lighting, no places of amusement, and no trace of excitement or life. The whole island was entirely absorbed in this one enterprise—quarrying and shipping superphosphate of lime. In fact, they ate it. They had to, because its amorphous dust permeated the air and settled on everything. One store seemed to sell all the island's requirements, including a very fiery and potent spirit.

There was little welcome for the hapless souls like ourselves stranded on these shores. The place was desolate, rocky and ugly. Our men spent most of their spare time trying to get used to the grog, but it remained their master to the end. The cook, a rank bad one at that, was so upset by it one day that he thought he was placing a tureen full of boiling hot pea-soup on our dining-table when in point of fact only a portion of the tureen was on, and it over-balanced, with disastrous results to the cook, for it scalded his bare feet. He jumped about the cabin in a frantic state yelling "Djavla Fan," which interpreted from Swedish means "the Devil in Hell"—which was true so far as he was concerned at the moment. The Captain was most annoyed, and gave him a sharp back-hander in the face in an effort to calm him; but he was far too under to be subdued by a blow.

8

ONE HUNDRED EGGS FOR A SHILLING

I was sent ashore to do some shopping for Sunday's dinner. The Dutchman in charge of the store thoroughly recommended his chicken, but I remarked we couldn't run to poultry—far too costly! I was dumbfounded when he said they were sixpence each, and eggs one shilling a hundred! I returned on board, much to everyone's amusement, with a score of emaciated cockerels over my shoulder and a hundred eggs in a bag. Chicken were almost a pest; they roamed about the island in their hundreds and thousands; they were claimed by the finder: but they were poor things, and really not worth sixpence each. The sailors used to get all the supplies they wanted in return for a plug or two of ship tobacco. When tobacco was running low, we used to crawl about the hedges after dark and feel for the roosting fowls. Each one secured in this manner found its way into the ship's galley. They placed about a dozen of hastily-plucked birds into a dixie. Boiled Fowl was frequently on the menu, with custard pudding to follow. There was also a

species of wild pig which, if you troubled to catch
one, belonged to you. He was a little black fellow
with an enormous head and a small tapering body.
He was most plentiful, too. We used to have great
fun charging through these pigs, cavalry fashion
on a quadruped with loppy ears, with a sack for
a saddle. When in full cry, one was fairly comfortably mounted, but at a trot the going was
difficult and painful.

It was just luck to round up good pigs, for they
all seemed the same size and colour—young and
old looked alike to us; but the natives knew.
Before we sailed we bought a dozen, hoping in
this way to secure the right sort, but as usual,
true to the luck of a sailor, we were fooled. We
decided to have a banquet half-way across the
Atlantic, but the pigs were so tough that the
ordinary sheath-knife of a sailor was useless as a
butchering implement. We had to use a stiletto
specially made for the job.

9

DIRTY WORK

The Captain and I were invited to spend a day
at our Agent's place a little way out, where rough
shooting and wild-goat stalking was arranged in
our honour. I was looking forward eagerly to a
day off, but either by accident or design I was
forgotten and left on the ship, which filled me
with utter disappointment. The occasion was
seized upon to put me through some special training of a most disagreeable nature. It was to clear
up and tidy the fore-peak, a dark dingy part of

the ship that never saw daylight and was rarely visited by anything except rats. My expression, when I came up for a breather and to see daylight, must have betrayed my thoughts. They were instantly noticed. "You needn't go down to the fore-peak again. I want you to come with me to inspect the bilges." The ballast was now out. The bilges are the space between the ship's outer and inner skin, so to speak, and there is always to be found a certain amount of filthy stagnant fluid which the pumps are unable to reach. This fluid swishes and swirls with each movement of the ship and remains there for months. The stench was enough to kill a lion. Having bailed as much as possible, I had to remove the solid matter with my two cupped hands. This chiefly consisted of decomposed rats, having reached the gelatinous stage, mixed with other vile rubbish. This type of job had greater disciplinary effect when given to do before a meal, they discovered. Someone had to do it, and it was as well that I should know how.

On the first stroke of eight bells, which indicated that an hour's respite was at hand, I came on deck, and, peering into the crystal-clear sea, I could see dozens of fish nibbling daintily at minute crustacæ which usually flourish on a ship's hull under the water line. Craning to get a better view of what was going on under the ship's counter, I slipped and fell overboard. Under normal conditions I could not come to much harm, and goodness knows I was in dire need of a bath at that moment, for I was begrimed beyond recognition. But unfortunately I knocked my head against the ship's side *en route*, which shook me

up a bit and gashed my forehead open. All the
ship's hands were at dinner; in fact the whole
island had gone to dinner, so there was no one
about to do anything to help. The only way to
regain the ship was to swim forward to the anchor
cable and shin up. I was just able to do this, and
so ended a most disagreeable morning.

The mail service of the island was much like
everything else there, "a happy-go-lucky affair."
A small coasting schooner was the mail boat, and
her time of arrival and departure was casual in
the extreme.

As the West-Country schooner was going direct
to Falmouth, we entrusted our letters to her, but
they were never posted. The tiny ship failed to
reach the other side of the Atlantic. Her name
was added to the long list of missing vessels.

There was one relic at Fort Zoutman which
gave the place a stamp of originality. At anchor in
a peaceful recess of this imperturbable harbour
lay an old wooden tug boat. This oddity's sole
duty was to attend to sailing ships within the
harbour. At other times it was a much-patronised
resting place for sea birds. Every available space
of its exposed parts was fringed by tiers of gulls
—yellow legs, red legs, black legs, grey legs; beaks
too of many bright hues embellished this quaint
clinker-built structure. It made up a pretty
picture. I consider the gull, as a family, and a
large one, to be the best proportioned and the
smartest turned out of all the sea birds, and the
closer it is examined the more beautiful it seems
to become.

About once a week there was a regular hulla-
baloo at this *coin de repos*. The tug used to get

up steam and prepare for duty, much to the annoyance of the birds. Owing to old age, the boilers could only stand a steam pressure sufficient to drive her at four knots. This misfortune circumscribed her activities considerably, and kept her virtually a prisoner. She dare not put her nose outside the harbour. That is why incoming vessels were met by a pilot cutter under sail, and manned by six stout-hearted oarsmen.

That awesome entrance, where the fast-running ocean current swept past, skirmishing on its way with the sharp teeth of sunken coral reefs, churning the sea into a state of angry agitation—these conditions were more than the tug's power could cope with. Pane and I, working on the topsail yard, were much amused watching this sooty travesty of steam power proceeding slowly towards the quay, where the schooner was waiting for her. Her engines, due to defective parts, uttered a wheezy sound, much like the breathing of a person suffering from asthma. She was followed and surrounded by clouds of wailing and screeching gulls. The ponderous pelicans, too, tumbled carelessly from high, and splashed the silent water around with much vigour. It was a characteristic setting of the harbour life of Aruba, and most picturesque. Soon the bows of the Fowey schooner broke away from the wharf. The drooping peak of her mainsail clattered to the hoist. Her crew of five brave Cornish men waved us their "so long." Having parted with the tug, she headed for the great ocean, and with her ensign flowing at the main she sailed serenely out of sight, never to reach her next port, or to be heard of after that day.

10

PIGS ABOARD

The last few days on the island were busy ones, reeving new ropes and bending winter sails, and striking the royal yards, in preparation for the stiff job ahead; and when we actually sailed the difference in the ship's speed and liveliness, under good canvas, was most marked.

We stood out towards the coast of Venezuela. We sailed well into the Gulf of Maracaibo, in order to benefit by the smooth water, to make adjustments to the rigging and jib-boom guys. There was early evidence, after an hour's pitching and tossing under whole sails, that the uneven distribution of cargo (for the complete load only occupied the middle portion of the ship and looked, from the main hatch, much like a rocky hillock of the volcanic variety) was causing a severe straining effect on the ship; but having made the necessary rigging and guy adjustments, the Captain hoped that the ship would adapt herself to the unusual strain without showing too much distress when we got to bad weather. We spent most of that day dodging to and fro in the Gulf of Maracaibo, and had a magnificent view of the great mountain range Sierra Nevada with peaks running up to eight thousand feet. We then headed for the gateway into the Atlantic, a narrow straits which divides the two large islands of Haiti and Porto Rico. It is called Mona Passage. Weathering Aruba, we passed a barquentine bound there from Rio, called the *Reigate*, hailing from Swansea. We were moored quite close to her at

Rio, but had no idea she was bound for the same fate.

I must say that legging it across the Caribbean under full sails with a refreshing breeze, was most enjoyable. The whole length of the ship was lashed night and day with a tepid spray, which was invigorating, for the very hot weather was then at its peak. I used to stand on the fo'c'sle head, with nothing on except dungaree slacks and a sombrero hat, arms outstretched, revelling in the misty showers and spray. But the pigs, which had been destined to live and die under the fo'c'sle head, by all appearances did not share my pleasure. The poor things were very seasick and quite unable to stand owing to the ship's constant pitching and rolling. If they dared to leave their pens, it always meant they had to be rescued before every bone in their body was broken by being dashed from one side to the other. At first it amused us to see them rolling rapidly to and fro, squealing loudly, but it very soon became more than obvious that it was nothing but torture to have brought them to sea. Hans and I were detailed to look after them. While the weather was fine we were able to devote the necessary time. They were fed regularly, and generally well cared for, and they got to know us quite well. In fact, one little fellow called "Nick," with whom I used to share my plum duff, would on very fine days trot after me round the decks, but if he saw someone else coming towards him he would bolt back for dear life, tumbling over several times before he got safely back to the farm. He could walk quite well with the vessel's slight rolling, but to gallop was quite out of the question.

The Caribbean is in reality a huge reservoir of warm sea, measuring roughly two thousand miles in length, five hundred to seven hundred miles across and nearly two miles in depth. It is the starting point of the Gulf Stream, and keeps it constantly supplied.

II

THE "LAW OF STORMS"

The sighting of the highlands of San Domingo under the lee and the little clump called Mona right ahead meant that a few more hours would see us on the great highway of the Western ocean, starting our lonely trail home. When outward bound, one feels that the African or South American continents are close at hand and the weather is always agreeable, and this feeling provides one with a certain amount of mental comfort; but in the Roaring Forties from the Good Hope to Australia, or on the run from Australia across the lower Pacific to the Horn, or across the North Atlantic, each with its span of thousands of miles of inhospitable tractless sea, there awakes in the breast of the bravest sailor a feeling of loneliness. Against this feeling, there is comfort and courage to be found only in a boundless faith in the Divine Ruler of man's destiny. Our Skipper used to say that the best pulpit from which to convert a real sinner was the deck of a small sailing ship during an ocean storm.

We had reached a spot north-east of Porto Rico known as the Porto Rico trench. It is the second deepest part of all the known seas of the universe, where the depth measures twenty-nine thousand feet, or just over five miles. The deepest part ever sounded is off the Philippines in the Pacific. This measures thirty-one thousand feet.

We were becalmed. The day was sunless and sultry. Not a ripple disturbed the surface of the oily grey sea. We all felt as though we were carrying heavy weights on our heads, and breathing seemed difficult. The Captain was in a fidgety and restless mood, spending most of his time running up and down the companion-way, tapping the barometer and scanning the horizon in turn. It was obvious that there was a load on his mind.

I peeped through the skylight, which was open, and saw he was reading *Law of Storms*. "Good God! a hurricane coming"—flashed through my mind. I ran to my friend Olaf, and asked him what he thought; and when I told him what I had seen, he said the conditions were identical with the approach of such a storm. While we were talking, the Skipper's voice rang out through his cupped hands, which gave no doubt as to the urgency of the command: "All hands on deck to shorten sail." The helm was lashed, and every one of us, the Captain included, was busily passing gaskets and double gaskets round each sail to make them secure.

Within a short while everything was ready. The only bit of canvas left on was one small storm sail, and if the storm came this would probably blow away like tissue paper. The naked masts and yards looked foreboding against the leaden sky. Galley and fo'c'sle were abandoned and battened down. All hands were posted round the mizzen rigging, where a length of rope could be swiftly passed round the body if the worst came. Olaf

and Johann were posted to the wheel, with a
lashing round each. Long crestless waves came
rolling on us from the Bahamas direction. The
Captain thought this was a good omen, for it might
have indicated that the storm was moving away,
rather than approaching our position. Every
minute was an hour, every hour was a day. Between
the creaking sound caused by the sailless yards
jerking from one side to the other, distant sounds
of rumbling thunder could be heard. This again
was interpreted as a good sign. My thoughts strayed
to the depth of water beneath us—five miles! I
shuddered.

But our hour was not yet at hand. By eight
bells of the first watch, the sky was bright with
twinkling stars, and a gentle breeze swept us
blithely towards the Sargasso Sea. The storm had
taken another direction; or, in other words, we
were not in its tack.

CHAPTER VI

STORMS

I

SEAWEED

THERE is no need to wait for excitement in a wind-jammer; you are not only on the sea, but in it and with it all the time. Interesting events and thrilling experiences seem to follow in rapid succession. Three days later, when dawn broke over our little world, we seemed as if we had been picked up from the sea during the night and dropped unceremoniously on a desert of gold, where not a vestige of ocean was visible even from the highest point of the masts. We were engulfed in the notorious seaweed of the Sargasso.

Of all the weird places imaginable, this assuredly is the strangest. Here was a sailing ship, under full canvas, sailing slowly along what appeared to be interminable furrows in a field of golden grain. Terrible stories have been told about ships being marooned in the Sargasso weed, and the crews starved to death in consequence, but our experience discredits such fallacious stories. For two days we pushed slowly through under a light enough breeze, without fear, experiencing no difficulties.

Each seaweed plant is about a foot or more in length. It sits perpendicularly in the sea, just

ROYAL MAIL LINES

Martinique

Mont Pelée Volcano, Martinique

Erupted in 1902, destroying St. Pierre and 34,000 souls

showing its head above the surface. The plants
are very tightly packed, but they subside with the
least resistance, only to fill in the space immediately the ship has passed through, so that the
ship's wake is not even seen.

The Sargasso Sea may roughly be termed the
back-water of the Atlantic. Its circulation is re-
stricted and controlled by the stronger ocean
currents on either side of it, with the result that it
becomes the receptacle for ocean debris.

The seaweed, nevertheless, serves an important
purpose, for into its thick forest flock numberless
fish to spawn. Here, in their tender days, they can
hide securely from the ravages of their enemies
until they are able to look after themselves. It can
be called the home of the flying fish, and it was a
strange sight to see these fascinating creatures
breaking through this yellow maze, careering into
the air and finally crashing into the seaweed out of
sight again.

Those of us who had not been there before were
busy cleaning bottles and placing a plant in each
to take home as a memento of this strange part of
the ocean. I often conjectured what the result
would be if we were caught in a storm just here.
Would each breaking sea that struck the ship hurl
many tons of weed on board and so eventually
weight the ship down until she got unmanageable?
I cannot conceive what measures could be taken
to deal with such a contingency at the height of a
storm by night.

Our inimitable cockney was very funny on the
subject; he did not mind so much the idea of
sliding down five miles into the imponderable
depth of the Porto Rico trench, if it was Fate's

H

desire, but he was very disconcerted and despondent at the thought of being first of all whipped to exhaustion by this tough and smelly weed, and finished off by being choked by it. No! the quicker he quit this —————— locality the better pleased he would be. . . .

2

TANTALISING CONDITIONS

Although we seemed to have passed through the huge continent of seaweed, we still ran into isolated stretches for some time. We came through areas of wildly-confused seas as well, and on one occasion we saw something very unusual. In the middle of breaking sea, a calm patch was observed. It rose from the horizon much like an island appearing from the depths, and then suddenly it disappeared again. It continued rising and falling with each billow. Strange atmospheric irregularities and an erratic barometer offered some explanation. It was thought that a cyclonic disturbance had quite recently visited the area, with the result that the force of the hurricane had whipped the seaweed into thick isolated patches—so thick that it resembled land.

There was one remark to be made in Aruba's favour. It would be difficult to find ten men in better fettle than we were. The surfeit of eggs, poultry, wild bacon, and a super-abundance of sweet potatoes and fresh fruit, fresh air and twelve hours' sleep every night, had brought a sparkle to our eyes and a freshness to our rotund and bronzed faces, which augured well for our chances to put up a good fight if we were tested by storm and sea.

Fifty-six days, however, elapsed before the perilous journey ended, and thirty of these days were spent in a constant struggle against adversity and the wild weather of the North Atlantic. Our experience was to be no food, no fires, not a vestige of comfort, wet through night and day with scarcely any restful sleep. Moreover, we were hounded continuously by an inherent feeling that the fierceness and ruthlessness of the mountainous seas, mercilessly pounding such a frail craft, must eventually win.

It took thirty days to cover the last fifteen hundred miles, and during that time we were hove-to for a total period of fourteen days. Although during the whole of these fourteen days the wind was blowing from a favourable direction, the force was such that the high seas, which prevailed under the circumstances, precluded any attempt at running before.

These conditions are very tantalising to a small heavily-laden ship. The seamanship shown on such occasions by these experienced and dour mariners undoubtedly made such crossings by small vessels possible during the winter months, and there is no doubt but that the difference between life and death in a storm is usually to be found in the judgment of the Captain. Many a good ship has disappeared with all hands when the judgment has erred on the side of over-anxiety to benefit by a following storm.

3

CAUGHT OUT

One day we were running before a strong breeze which, had it been accompanied by a leaden sky and driving rain, would have been treated with much respect, but as the sun was shining brightly the Captain allowed the conditions to blind his judgment.

With the coming of night and an increase in the force of the wind, he realised that we should have shortened sail and hove-to before nightfall. He stayed on deck all through the night. He was on occasions alarmed at the ferociousness of the following sea, which lifted the old craft's stern feet into the air and then hurled her along at a terrific and almost uncontrollable speed, dashing first to port, many degrees off her course in a bewildered fashion, then screwing back an equal amount to starboard in a most perilous manner, heeding little to the helmsman's frantic efforts to keep her steady.

Seas were toppling inboard in the main rigging on both sides in turn, and the decks resembled the rapids of Niagara. We seemed to be running helter-skelter to the devil. The men thought that we had fallen into the most perilous of all the storm traps known to sailors. No attempt could be made to free ourselves until daylight, and even then could we escape, or had we gone too far?

At midnight it was decided to take in the main top-gallant sail and fore upper-top sail, and to reef the fore-sail. During these operations, I was sent to the wheel, the Skipper keeping an eye on me, but it was much too big a job for one so inexperienced. In a second she broached to. I had failed to anticipate and check a heavy yaw, and she ran along the trough between two huge seas like a terrified rabbit. For a while she seemed perfectly motionless, heeling over dangerously to leeward. Providentially, all hands were on the fore-yard and momentarily out of danger.

What a sight they must have had, and what a fright, as they saw a gigantic sea on the beam collecting strength and determination and speed ere it crashed over us with unmitigated fury, completely submerging the entire main-deck and wrenching the lifeboat on the main-hatch from the chain grips and jamming it between the fo'c'sle and lee fore-rigging! The cascade continued its irresponsible career, filling the fo'c'sle and galley and smashing the temporary bulkhead that we had erected under the fo'c'sle head to give the pigs their only partition and protection between them and a watery grave.

It was a sad stock-taking that took place when order was more or less restored. A bedraggled party crept round in the dim light of a hurricane lamp. The decks were littered with smashed fragments of lifeboat, hencoops, and odd bits of timber. In the scuppers floated from one side to the other the remains of what was once our livestock. All the fowls had gone, and with the exception of two which were jammed in debris under the bowsprit, the pigs too had disappeared, including my little Nick. The two grunting survivors appeared little the worse for the experience. They were put below in the fore-peak, out of harm's way. They were actually due on the table in two days' time.

With the strengthening of the sun on the morrow the rough sea died down considerably, and our log reading at noon gave an excellent twenty-four hours' run of over two hundred miles. We decided to kill the two pigs before they died of broken hearts.

4

PIGS FOR DINNER

It was a great disappointment to us all that in spite of enjoying favourable conditions across the Carribean, through the Sargasso and along the Gulf Stream, well up into the higher latitudes, our livestock utterly failed to appreciate it.

The fowls, that had been given an excellent home in the old lifeboat on the main-hatch, certainly presented us with a few eggs for the first week or two, but after that they seemed to lose all interest in life. Their dishevelled feathers fell off, one by one, to disclose an ill-nourished carcass and to crush any hopes that we had cherished of relishing roast fowl at a time on the passage home when such a dish would have been worth its weight in gold, and would have carried us on for days. I must add, also, that though we did get a few eggs, they did not fit in at all well with weevily ship's biscuits, and they were generally looked upon as a disappointment. Even when added to boiled rice, they seemed to make a ghastly mess of the rice.

The pigs were in a worse plight even than the fowls. They had found the hard wet decks and the constant movement very trying, and the galley ashes in their pens were a poor substitute for the soil and freedom of their native bush. They seemed quite unable to get their sea legs, and when the few root crops which we had brought for them had been eaten up, they, like ourselves, had to be content to fall back for their staple diet on the hard and uninteresting ship's biscuits. These they tired

of, and as time went on they would nose them out
of the trough on to the bare deck, when they
would be washed away by the sea. We could see
the old boatswain's words coming true, and his
cynical sneer was gradually changed into a sarcastic smile as he watched these poor brutes
getting thinner and thinner.

We decided to prepare the pigs for the worst.
No one seemed ready to answer the call for volun-
teers to kill them. Olaf and Pane were pressed,
and eventually decided to try. The layman might
think that such a job is not fraught with any
difficulty, but believe me, it was a terrible business,
because to the uninitiated there did not seem to
be a starting point to the butchery. The process
became in fact so involved that one pig got away
when he had been manœuvred into a most advantageous position and operations had commenced on
him. Olaf suggested that he had earned his liberty.
Better results were obtained when a home-made
stiletto was used on him. The skin was much
too tough to be pierced by the ordinary sheath
knife.

We had worked ourselves up to a high pitch of
excitement during the cooking ceremony. Many
visits were made to the galley door. An excellent
aroma escaped from the stove. An atmosphere of
home was evident when the oven door was opened
for basting purposes. Sizzling jets of fat shot into
space like miniature rockets. All this looked very
good, but when the pigs were trimmed ready for
cooking, heads cut off for brawn, and so on, they
looked surprisingly small, and having been roasted
for a couple of hours they were smaller still. The
feast was equally divided; one pig went aft and the

other to the fo'c'sle. The longed-for meal, however, was a complete fiasco. So tough were the pigs that they completely defied the carver's skill. Rather than starve we treated ourselves to chunks of crackling.

Brawn had been promised for tea. There might have been a little hope in this direction, we thought, but when the cabin's share was knocked out of the bully tin in which it had been placed for pressing purposes, the first thing I saw on my side of the brawn, as it sat on a tin plate, was a black hairy ear. The Captain gazed at a nostril, while my *vis-à-vis* counted a row of teeth. Apparently the head had been boiled whole, and that was brawn. There had been a slight misunderstanding as to the difference between a pig's head and what the English people call a "pig's head" when specially prepared. The cook thought that the tin part of the business, and the pressing, was just ritual. However, despair drove us to find quite luscious bits in this unsightly mess; and much was forgiven.

That brought to an end our farming experience; and when it was remembered that these pigs and fowls had taken the major share of our food for nearly a month, we had not made much profit.

Yes! Old Bristly was right; small ships made poor farms, and sailors in them worse farmers.

5

BOW ON

I have often been asked how these small vessels survive these terrible storms, when large five-thousand-ton steamers like the *Usworth* and *Mill-pool* are sent to their doom, as these two were in the North Atlantic recently, taking with them in each instance all hands. Once a steamship is unable, either through a breakdown of machinery or of steering gear, to maintain a relative position to the sea that is safe, then she has nothing else to rely on. She soon becomes broad-side on, her whole length is then subjected to the wrathful bombardment of the sea. A few minutes of this, however big the ship might be, if the waves are really angry, suffices to pound her to pieces.

A sailing vessel has the great advantage that she can retain her prow-on position by sail-trimming, and remain in that position even without touching the helm for days and nights on end. When a sailing vessel is hove-to, her strongest part, her shoulders, so to speak, and the most buoyant part as well, face the onslaught. Her sails are reduced, so that her speed is just enough to keep her in that steady position and under control. Every time a wave breaks against this buttress she is hurled back; in other words, she recedes with the blow, just as a clever boxer evades the full force of his opponent's punch by receding. Providing the sea does not batter its way through some weak spot in her superstructure into the interior, she is as safe as a house.

There are other contingencies that might cause disaster, but they are remote, such as colliding with unseen obstacles like floating wreckage or a derelict vessel, or hitting an iceberg; or the wind might suddenly die away altogether at the height of a storm, leaving the vessel without sail control. Then her head pays off, and if she falls broadside on into the trough, two or three waves will come over, and she is no more.

The brig *Excelsior*, that I once sailed in, nearly succumbed to this fate. She was also by a coincidence sailing from Aruba. The first sea that struck her consequent to her losing her bow-on position carried away everything on her deck, including all her bulwarks from stem to stern. This latter damage was providential and ultimately saved her, for all subsequent waves that came over were like sea running over a half-tide rock. The *Excelsior* limped into Falmouth much the worse for wear but with personnel unharmed. This was a miracle, for the men must have clung on to the ship like monkeys after the bulwarks had been carried away.

On another occasion we only narrowly missed colliding with a large raft of heavy balks, chained together, which had evidently broken loose from a tug on the American side of the Atlantic. On another trip we owed our escape from being entangled in the deathly embrace of one of those ocean ghosts known as derelicts, by a rain squall clearing up just in time to reveal her position close under our bows. She chased us twice off our course.

6

FIVE HUNDRED TONS OF SEA

Our arrival in the storm areas was heralded in no uncertain manner. Although through the night we had been pounding along before a stiffish breeze, it was not until dawn that we discovered that things were definitely looking ugly. The sky was heavy with fast-moving clouds scudding at a low altitude, and the sea was rapidly getting bigger and more vicious. It was an eerie atmosphere.

The Captain looked apprehensive as he told the two watches to get breakfast over quickly. He wanted all hands to remain on deck to put the ship under storm sails and make all preparations to heave-to. Breakfast had to be cut short. Boatswain came down to the cabin to report that conditions were suddenly much worse, and that the wind was increasing in force and accompanied by blinding rain.

It was apparent that vile conditions had been existing in this latitude for some time, as the seas were quite out of proportion to the amount of wind that we had been having, but within an hour they were both fairly evenly matched and very nasty.

The manœuvre of heaving-to in such a sea was a haunting thought. It seemed almost an impossible feat for a vessel of this size, loaded down to her deck, to achieve; but it was attempted and done.

All hands looked anxious as they were ordered to climb many feet up the mizzen-rigging. Here we would be clear of the danger of being washed overboard in the event of a sea being shipped when broad-side on. The only man to remain on deck was Olaf. He was chosen as the most experienced A.B. to take charge of the wheel. To that he was lashed securely. We were filled with admiration as we gazed down on this solitary figure, cut off from the rest of his companions. His weather-beaten face was set with an expression of grim determination to carry out the job that he had been appointed to do.

The Captain, who had climbed some distance above us, had arranged a series of visual signals with Olaf, who could not hear his voice through the gale. From this high position (as he was above the seas and could compare their height) he was thus the better able to discriminate and to decide on the propitious moment to bring the ship to. What a time of dreadful responsibility! But his mind was made up for him in double-quick time. A large sea could be seen towering above the others, tearing after us like a maddened monster seeking prey. So far, the old ship had behaved most excellently, except that the steering was erratic, which caused her to ship heavy lumps in the region of the main chains on both sides. But this wave chasing us was apparently a forerunner of a series of bigger ones, as the wind was now moderate gale force. And as it was full gale force in the squalls, the indications were that much worse conditions were close at hand.

When skimming through the trough of the preceding sea, it was evident that something serious must happen. Amid the din of roaring torrent and the howling of the wind, the Captain's voice shrieked: "We are going to have it! It's coming! Look out!"

Poor Olaf. It was not difficult to imagine his feelings as he saw through the corner of his eye five hundred tons of infuriated ocean scowling spitefully at him from the skies, and gathering strength to pounce on him, to remind him that men who come to sea in ships, to conjure with the tempest, do so at their peril.

The *Pride of Wales* made a gallant effort to reach the top, but being so heavily laden and her speed

greatly reduced, she was more or less at the mercy
of big seas like this.

Down it came, crash! hitting us slightly on the
port quarter.

The poop-deck was completely submerged. The
ship's timbers shivered ominously. Olaf's head
peeped over after a while, but in the boiling and
seething mass he seemed complacent enough, and
took it as his share.

The ship had now been lifted to almost a perpendicular angle. Her stern was high in the air, which
caused the cascade to career the whole length of
the main deck. Pane, the cockney, yelled in my
ear: "Another of those and we needn't bother to
go down on deck."

But ships and sailors must enjoy a surfeit of
good luck to carry them through their perilous
existence, and on this occasion it came our way.
The ship now had broached-to partially on her
own account, so that before more trouble arrived
we were able to bring her nose to the storm.

Riding out a gale in this way is a monotonous
business. A three hundred-ton vessel is small
enough when it is possible to use all the accommodation that her size admits, but on these occasions
we were huddled together on the poop-deck,
which incidentally was the most exposed part of
the ship. There we were grouped, pinned, and
tethered in a standing position against the rigging
or a mast, ducking the head continuously to avoid
the full force of a whack in the face from a chunk
of sea blown by the gale.

To hold the body, poised uncomfortably on
relaxed and limp knees, was the only method of
retaining balance and counteracting the jerky move-

ments of this storm-tossed coracle. Driving rain, too, soon found its way between the neck and muffler to make doubly sure that the discomfort was complete. But perhaps the worst suffering was caused through the constant hissing and shrieking of the wind round one's very brain— not a moment's respite—everlastingly on, the process went. I thought it must eventually drive us all mad. It seemed to chisel its way into one's head. This was a torture in itself.

We had to make frequent sorties to man the pumps. Even all this would have been tolerable if, when the watch below came, comfort, warmth, and food were at hand; but after a few hours of storm conditions, cooking has to be abandoned through the sheer impossibility of keeping a fire going. A sailor's stock of clothing, too, is soon exhausted, with the result that he has no chance of a change after two or three days of bad weather. Some of the bunks, by virtue of position, may be fairly dry, but as a general rule bed and bed-clothing suffer the same fate as wearing apparel. Human endurance knows no measure in small deep-sea sailing ships.

During the night the fo'c'sle was out of bounds, as heavy seas pounded these parts continuously. The lazaret was made as comfortable as conditions would permit; besides, it kept all hands in the after-part of the ship, in case urgent orders were issued. Several old sails were brought there from the sail locker for'ard. This was done by carrying these through the hold, and it was the devil's own job to tramp over a rough cargo with the ship describing every angle that Euclid had invented.

Old sails are snug things to sleep on; they are so clean and serve both purposes, bedding and bed-

clothes, and there are plenty to go round. At eight
that night I was sent below and told not to come on
deck again until dawn. I threw myself down without removing my soaking wet oilskins and clothes,
and prayed to Almighty God to show His mercy
on us. Sleep was out of the question. Several times
I staggered to the top of the companion-way,
hoping that someone would come that I could speak
to. I tried to force my way out, but it was secured
from the outside. I slithered from one side of the
cabin to the other like a drunkard. A suspended
paraffin lamp in the skylight had not been trimmed
that day. It was gradually dying out, and the night
was not yet half through. If left alone in the dark
I felt I would die. The ship appeared on occasions
to be falling long distances through hideous space.
I could hear the Captain's voice saying it was one
of the worst storms he had experienced. This was
meagre comfort to me. I was much cheered when
later he yelled, "What a fine sea-boat she is!"

Dawn revealed a sight never to be forgotten,
and I was allowed to go on deck and move about
with the others, but with limited freedom, of
course. The first impression I got was that a titanic
battle was raging between one of the greatest and
most powerful laws of Nature and the wit of man,
with the human putting up an extraordinarily good
performance. To design a craft not only capable
of challenging such conditions with an even chance
of success, but to do so carrying a handicap weight
of excessive proportions, speaks highly of the
ship's design and equally highly of the personnel
manning it.

For three days and three nights we climbed
these ocean slopes with monotonous regularity.

Our sole surface companion was that sprightly little creature the Stormy Petrel, skimming the huge waves, lilting happily in his nimble stride; and when things looked black and the chances of seeing another dawn were remote, how I longed to change places with him! I used to watch him with great interest, and one marvelled where such mites stored their inexhaustible energy. They never seem to rest or to want to. They are the only winged creatures of the heavens that venture so far out into the wilds of the great oceans. Even at mealtime he does not think it necessary to enjoy it under restful conditions. He searches for his dainty bit with much vigilance and vigour, twisting sharply this way and that, and when it is eventually sighted he approaches it tripping lightly on the seas much like a ballet girl tip-toeing the stage. This artistic performance continues until the meal is over. Then he rushes off to catch up with the ship. He seems loth to miss a single phase of the struggle going on between the ship and the storm. Even in the depths of night his tiny form could be detected skimming over the foamy wake—still following, still flying on. Sailors are superstitious folk, and the behaviour of this little bird causes them much perplexity. They ask why he is the only bird seen in these distant and desolate parts, often a thousand miles from his rocky home. Why is he so interested in ships, and why does he seem to intensify that interest when the ship is fighting for her existence? If he intended to land and make use of the ship to rest his tiny wings, much could be understood, but he doesn't—he is not known to perch on any part of a ship. Does he follow for dietetic reasons?

No! he is not in the least attracted by anything a
ship has to offer in that respect. He will not
trouble to turn his head to look at chunks that may
be thrown to him in the form of food. Sailors,
due to the banishment that is associated with the
life, welcome and enjoy the companionship of
creatures indigenous to ocean life. It is a change
from looking at shipmates whose begrimed and
bearded faces have ceased to be a novelty. But
they do not like the Stormy Petrel.

His presence is conspicuous in stormy weather.
He appears on those occasions to be so thoroughly
interested that sailors believe he has an uncanny
attachment ·to any disaster that might befall men
of the sea. Some think, too, that this undemon-
strative little bird represents the re-incarnation of
those who have perished at sea, and that he is
anxious to see the liberation of as many souls as
possible, in order to perpetuate his genus. He
received the name Petrel, which is a corruption
of Peter, the Saint, because of his ability to walk
on the sea.

On the fourth day a respite came, and it lasted
only just long enough for us to get the fires going
to cook some much-needed food and to dry our
clothing and bedding. The original fo'c'sle, which
was below deck for'ard, was turned into a drying-
room, and the little buggy stove was kept at
red-hot heat. But what a swamp; yet sailors had
made it their home for over twenty years.

Those were hard days. More heavy weather
was in store; and this time we made no mistake,
for we hove-to in ample time and made everything
as snug as possible. It was good prophecy, for in
the middle of that night conditions once more were

awful. Gusts of hurricane force swept down on us from west-north-west, with cold sleet showers to make them more disagreeable.

Two days later, we saw under our lee a barque, also hove-to. She was about four miles away, but we saw her only occasionally when both happened to be cresting a sea at the same time. She was, we thought, of Scandinavian origin, for she possessed that most useful adjunct only common to vessels from the North-European countries, a large windmill, which was used with excellent effect for pumping purposes. The windmill whizzed round gaily. How at that very hour we longed to have one! So far as we could gather, she was not doing any worse than we were, although some of her storm-sails were tattered. It is of course an impossible task to tidy up these things at the height of a storm. Both vessels were on the port tack, so there was no danger of getting into each other's way. There is nothing more disturbing than two vessels closing in on each other in a storm on different tacks. The unfortunate ship whose duty it is to give way runs great risk of being swamped in attempting to obey the rules of the road. That night the wind backed several points, and we were lucky to see another dawn. We took frightful punishment, due mainly to the change in the direction of the sea following late after the change of wind.

When daylight came, we scanned the horizon in vain for our companion of the previous day. What her fate was we could never know, but a fairly accurate conjecture could be made. We must have drifted over the spot where she took her final plunge. Such is the irony of fate. It cast a gloom over us all, for we began to wonder if

she was in distress the day before and was unable
to communicate the fact to us. It was all very
difficult, and a physical impossibility to train a
telescope or binoculars on her long enough to discern her state. Even if we had actually known that
she was in distress, so wild were the weather conditions, and terrific the seas, that it would have
been practically impossible to carry out a manœuvre that would result in rendering those hapless
souls effective assistance.

7

BATTERIES OF HELL

During a falling off in the force of the wind and
a brightening up generally, which proved to be
a wolf in sheep's clothing, we had a further exciting
time. It was found necessary to set two more sails,
in order to check a most disagreeable roll that was
responsible for much sea being scooped inboard
on the weather side. The two sails selected were
the double-reefed mizzen-stay sail and the fore
top-mast stay sail.

The former was easily set, but the latter, being
in an exposed position on the bowsprit, required
rather expert handling, for it was still blowing hard
enough, and this part of the ship was continuously
under water, and from the poop looked bleak and
dangerous. Johann was sent out, having been
secured with a life-line at the other end of which
were the Chief and two A.B.s.

The head of the ship was paid off as much as
was deemed safe. Johann mounted the fo'c'sle head
and carefully crept out, watched anxiously by us

all. The danger was that he might be dashed against the ship's bows; but he had the satisfaction of knowing that his body at least would be retrieved. He was twice dipped out of sight, but he clung on tenaciously. But the third time the lower part of his body floated away, and he was thrown over the bowsprit on his back, yet he recovered from a tangle of gear little the worse.

The addition of these two small sails made a great difference, not only to our comfort, but to the ship's comfort also, and Johann had done a good job of work.

Soon after dark one or two stars peeped through a bewildered sky, and winked at us, but failed to fool us.

8

AN EERIE NIGHT

There was much evidence that the demon storm was preparing to give us another good hiding. Wintry conditions had closed on us with a sudden vengeance. In a few hours the temperature had fallen almost to freezing point. The wind, too, was now running round the compass, staying nowhere long.

Black, angry clouds wrote their warning on the walls of the heavens as they sped past. The ship was rolling and labouring heavily. Her head had been dragged through every point of the compass in as many minutes. Desultory lumps of sea fell all round the deck with their ominous thuds. The silhouettes of seamen could be seen swinging to and fro against a sombre sky. They were aloft, goose-winging the main lower-top sail. This is a

term applied to a process which reduced considerably the canvas area of this small storm-sail.

Was Captain Griffith preparing his little charge
for the fight of her life? If barometer pressure was
any indication, he most certainly was. He paced
the poop in a quick and restless manner. His
silence betrayed a mind overloaded with anxiety.
It required little additional evidence to persuade
us that soon we would be in the track of a storm
of unequalled fury, but we got much.

Storms, like plays, are staged with much garnish
and glitter, and on this occasion nothing seemed
to have been left out in an effort to produce a
masterpiece.

Three hours of the first night watch were spent
studying the elements with mingled curiosity and
much misgiving. Balls of living flame danced on
the extremity of each yard and mast; the rigging,
too, was streaked with an uncanny fire. Each
flame crackled its defiance of our presence in these
wilds.

The strange phenomenon is known to the sailor
as Jack-o'-lantern, and he hates to see it because
it usually spells ill for his safety and comfort.
These balls of fire are actually the result of electric
discharges frequently found in a stormy atmosphere.
They are fired, so the scientists say, by warm air
currents. Favourable conditions for the firing of
these charges are evidently to be found at the
extremity of yards and tops of masts and exposed
parts of rigging of ships.

We looked odd in the extreme, and might have
been taking part in an illuminated ocean gymkhana.

In the small hours of the morning we were
struck by a heavy squall. It caught us all aback;

but it did not take us long to get the right side of
it. The much-dreaded hour had come. Although
there was a lull after the first onslaught, it settled
down. By eight bells of the middle watch we were
in the throes of a storm with wind of hurricane
force. It seemed as though all the batteries of hell
had got our range. It blew from the north-west,
and this quarter well knows how to produce a
tempest. On this occasion it rose to prodigious
heights. Wind of immeasurable force straight off
the ice of Greenland's mountains, laden with bullets
of frozen rain, tore against our faces, roaring
thunder shook the very ship beneath us, and lightning of spectacular intensity blinded us.

A sea which had been lashed to colossal dimensions threw itself about in wild confusion. All
these combined in a crescendo of frightfulness
and continued throughout the darkness of the
night, culminating in a raging inferno.

Those of the duty watch were huddled in a
cramped position under the lee of the mizzen-
mast; a small canvas dodger was fixed here. We were
lashed to the pumps every hour. The sea rushed
to and fro with a deafening roar, often reaching
as high as our shoulders. Here we had to wring
from our neglected and ill-nourished bodies the
energy necessary to deal with the sea that was
gushing through the seams of the ship's weather-
beaten and strained sides. The watch below was
again brought to the lazaret, where they dosed
in their wet clothes.

This small ship, for she looked smaller than ever
in the midst of these gigantic seas, was putting
up a splendid fight. The three sails were tugging
in earnest at their sheets and kept her well in posi-

tion. As a matter of fact, were it not for anxiety lest anything untoward should happen, we could have all gone below, except when pumping time came round.

Pangs of hunger and numbed limbs were our greatest enemies. Although on such occasions tea and coffee could be prepared with difficulty, serious cooking was out of the question, and in consequence we were rapidly becoming weak.

When the storm was at its height we saw a grand spectacle—a large American liner coming up under our lee. She was a vessel of about eight thousand tons. Between the wild gusts we watched her come over the horizon. For a long time only her white superstructure and funnels could be seen, and they only occasionally. She was westward bound and was steaming at about quarter speed, somewhere about four knots, straight into the storm. We were making much better weather of it than she appeared to be. Quite frequently she buried her bows as far as the fore part of the bridge completely, and threw columns of sea over the top of the funnels, which were blanched with brine. What a sight! She appeared much interested in seeing us, and was inclined to be chatty, but we were not of the same mood. It is quite impossible to carry on code conversations from the deck of a small vessel in such weather; but she seemed to understand when we ran our ensign up, which meant that we were at least alive. She replied with a hoist, wishing us well, and later dipped her ensign.

We were able to catch a glimpse of the sun on the next day; and were surprised, when our position was worked out, to find that we had drifted in eleven days many hundreds of miles nearer home. The Gulf Stream was responsible for a great portion of this drift, and the lee way for the remainder. It must be remembered that a sailing vessel when hove-to makes little or no headway, but she goes to leeward at a great pace.

Five hundred miles from the chops of the Channel sounded cheerful, but four days of strong easterly wind brought us no nearer. The little vessel was leaking so badly through the hammering she had received during the last ten days that she refused to be driven against even a moderate head sea, so that nothing but a favourable wind was of any use, and not too much of that.

The Captain remarked: "Another crossing like this would be her finish." He was wrong. She completed two more winter crossings. But she went down on the third.

Nearing the Channel was more than exciting; we seemed back in civilisation. Steamers and sailing vessels criss-crossed in every direction. We picked up the loom of the Lizard light, forty-five miles away. A look-out had been posted in the bunt of the fore-yard. I was there with him when a faint reflection lighted the eastern horizon, but it was not reported until we could time the flashes in the sky accurately. It was no mistake; the powerful Lizard light could be seen right ahead. Wonderful navigation by these men o' sail. By eleven o'clock that night it was reminiscent of walking up Piccadilly, with Eros in the Circus as our goal. We were surrounded by flashing, revolving, and flicking lights.

After the prosaic life we had led since leaving Rio, our heavy hearts and empty stomachs were much cheered. Although the night was very dark, the firmament was bewitched with lustrous and twinkling stars, and as we scudded along with slanting keel, luffing up towards the Devon coast, our thoughts strayed with a longing desire to wake those dear and near to us with a loving embrace.

At break of the fiftieth day since leaving Aruba, we had the first glimpse of dear old England. The tall white mast of Lloyd's signalling station on Prawle Point welcomed us with the answering pennant at the dip, which meant that he was inviting us to report, and wishful for our name. Having hoisted our numbers and requested that our ship's husband be informed, we kept away up Channel, before a fresh breeze from over the land, and a calm sea.

We arrived off Harwich two days later, just before dark. So close in were we, that people walking about were plainly visible. It was most tantalising, for it was obvious that the pilots were in no mood to reply to our signal that night, to conduct us into safety. The wind, which had been blowing freshly over the land, suddenly backed to south-east, and by nine o'clock that night we were caught in a raging blizzard, with wind of hurricane force. This was the cruellest of all blows; and with the wind from that direction it was one of the most dangerous parts of the English coast to be at, a lee shore.

To add to our confusion, a wretched light-ship called the *Galloper*, denoting one of the most treacherous sandbanks at the mouth of the Thames estuary, had apparently had its light altered from red to green, and this since we were last in any port, so that we had no knowledge of the change.

We spent an appalling night trying to get away from the many dangers lurking all round. Heavy canvas had to be carried continuously with the result that all our old games of the wilds of the Atlantic had to be started over again.

But this time we had additional terrors to contend with—sandbanks and a congestion of shipping which, owing to the blinding sleet, could only be seen occasionally.

The short seas of the North Sea were much more troublesome and distressing than the mountainous ones of the open ocean. While one was thumping on our bows, another was engaged filling our deck amidships, while a third gave us its parting benediction just in front of the wheel, completely blinding the helmsman. This went on without cessation for two whole days. We were well on the way towards the Dogger Bank.

On the fifty-sixth day we had returned to our old position off Harwich, and, thank God! we were seized by a vulturous tug which dragged us up the river to Ipswich. Reduced to a point of starvation and our strength ebbing rapidly, we all dropped to sleep as we stood, leaving the old pilot to carry on with the job of steering in the wake of the tug.

It seemed a fitting day and time to end our voyage—we docked on Sunday to the chimes of the morning service.

9

SIMPLY ABOUT FOOD

Many curious people, who had heard that we had been seen off Harwich the night the great storm descended, which covered the whole of the British Isles and had caused enormous havoc to shipping, came to see us dock. Many vessels had been lost with all hands, and the North Sea fishing fleet had suffered heavily.

Longshoremen jumped on board to help us with the mooring hawsers and chains, and we were thankful, for we had little strength left for heavy work. Our faces and hands were chapped to a point of laceration, and were very painful.

The old ship, too, was in a sad plight. A few remaining shreds of the top gallant sails hung from the yards. They had been hurriedly furled on the night of the storm and were blown to bits in no time. What remained of the lifeboat on the main hatch told its own story of stormy days, while a big rent in the bulwarks from the fore to the main rigging gaped over the dock sides.

The Captain, in a sporting manner, challenged me to go ashore and return with a good dinner for all hands. He gave me a chit on the ship's agents up to £1 in value.

I found walking very difficult. It always is so when one has been tossed about at inconceivable angles for many weeks on end; one's legs refuse to function properly. But tacking up a narrow cobbled lane leading from the dock, I was guided by a delicious smell of cooked food to a half-open door of a bakehouse. Here I found the proprietor of a cooked-meat shop getting ready for Monday's trading. I told him my story, and showed him my warrant. He seemed much touched, and took me to the house, where he immediately made me hot tea and also presented me with a large meat pie, which I devoured voraciously and instantly.

He drew me to tell him more of our experiences, and as there was a chance that this might help me along with my mission, I continued. He appeared most sympathetic, and promised to come with me to the ship when his family returned from church, so that he could gauge our requirements more accurately.

To kill time I meandered along the narrow way and reached what looked like an important thoroughfare. Being Sunday and church time, it was deserted, and the quietness made me feel curiously out of place. I was obsessed with an idea that I was trespassing. This is a complex that the captivity, rigid discipline, and that constant suppression to which the sailor-in-making is subjected to, suffers from.

Leaning against a shop window to rest my comic sea-legs, I ruminated amid the strange surroundings. I was half expecting to find the highway rollicking along and throwing spume and spray in my face. I was quite unable to accommodate my confused and storm-tossed brain to the monumental rigidity of the buildings. If they had only rolled a little they would have seemed natural.

The monotony was broken by the approach of a burly policeman. I was half afraid of him. Would my neglected appearance attract his attention? It was quite likely that it would, for I looked an unmitigated outcast. But he was a kindly soul, and seemed pleased to have someone to talk to. He asked me where I came from. I said—the Dock. "I can see that," he said, "but what part of the world?" I replied "Aruba." "Where is that?" "In the West Indies." "Hum! You seem to have had some sunshine there." "Yes, plenty."

"What are you doing here?" I replied, "I am waiting for some food for the ship's company." "So you are hungry, are you?" "Yes, very."

Having unravelled my story about the cookshop, he was apparently satisfied and left, wishing me luck. I followed slowly in his wake for a time, until I was arrested by the strains of sacred music which filled the air, the first that I had heard since I had left home. It was soothing; it was beautiful. It came from an imposing-looking church close by. There was suddenly a stir. Carriages, with their cockaded coachmen, and well-groomed horses jingling the frothy bit, lined the pavement. The doors of the church opened and the music became louder. The worshippers, warmly clad in furs and overcoats, filtered out of the church into the chill November air. I was deeply interested watching this fashionable gathering chatting happily and sauntering homewards, where I could visualise a table covered with good things, and cosy fires waiting to greet them.

I suddenly became conscious that someone had noticed my strange appearance. Feeling full of shame, I fled down a narrow side-street, which brought me to the dock, and once more to my rightful atmosphere.

I returned to the bakehouse simultaneously with the baker's family. So well did he repeat my story to his wife that she expressed the desire to come down with us to the ship to see for herself, and to do· anything she could to help. It was a most fruitful visit, and they both went out of their way to play the part of the Good Samaritan. Their own meal was put back until our galley was stocked to capacity with hot meat pies, fruit tarts, milk, butter, eggs and other things of great worth. So interested were they that they stayed in the ship and talked to us while we guzzled their ware. I won approbation from all hands. Few of them thought, as they saw me disappear over the ship's side, that I should have had such a successful morning. And they had reason to be sceptical, for we were penniless, which was perhaps the most serious handicap, and it was Sunday, when all the business places were closed; and lastly, there was my appearance, which could have done little towards creating an atmosphere of confidence.

But Luck turns up sometimes to aid the disconsolate, and it certainly came my way that day. I later took a bundle of wet clothes to the bakehouse, where they soon dried before the roaring fire, so that the last day of my first voyage ended quite happily.

CHAPTER VII

SECOND VOYAGE

I

A NEW VOYAGE

RETURNING from a most happy leave, I found the journey from Portmadoc to Ipswich very trying. I picked the Captain up at Barmouth, and we travelled overnight. The only difference between our mental conditions due to home-sickness was that whereas the tears ran silently down his cheeks, mine were accompanied by bitter and loud sobs. My feelings were much worse than on the first voyage. I knew this time what was in store for me, and I could not see a ray of hope of any pleasing novelty. The thought that we were to spend our Christmas at sea was sad indeed. At home the presents were being bought, and Christmas cards were busily arriving, and yet I was leaving it all, to commune with Life's roughest and most inhospitable elements, to live with men I knew not and who would probably be entirely out of sympathy with my life and feelings; to serve another indefinite term in captivity.

That was my unhappy self travelling to the *Pride of Wales* for my second voyage with her.

This second voyage was not so eventful as the first one. I shall therefore not describe it in detail, but shall take from my diaries scenes and episodes which were not covered in the first voyage, thus adding to the rounded whole of my sea experience and to the tale of the little beauty, the *Pride of Wales*. This time she was bound for two French islands in the West Indies, half cargo for each, Martinique and Guadaloupe.

2

THE NEW CREW

This voyage was remarkable for its crew. I must first describe their arrival. They were signed on the day before we sailed, and the Captain was much impressed by their appearance; but only one turned up that day, and this was most awkward, as we were sailing early in the morning. We knew what this meant—farewell parties and much merry-making, Christmas cheer and fare days in advance!

The next morning found the dock gates opened; the heavily-laden ship was warped to the pier head in readiness for the tug to make fast. The weather was bitterly cold. Snow lay deep over all and a biting north-east wind swept the heavens. There was little comfort in a small sailing ship on such a day. The cook was one of the delinquents; in consequence, there were no organised meals.

The air was rent from time to time by impatient blasts from the tug's siren. Would that they came!

A handful of morbid people with red noses and shrivelled forms stood above us on the quay. What they could see to interest them, it was difficult to surmise—they certainly supplied additional atmosphere to an already tragic picture.

At last, here they came! The rumbling wheels

of a vehicle and the patter of horses' hoofs echoed round the dock. A moment later a comic-looking conveyance hove in sight. It was groaning with kitbags, sea-chests, and humans—yes, they had arrived. The Captain, who meantime had been working up towards the limit of his endurance, suddenly relaxed—his frowns turned into smiles. The sight of these breezy, jovial, light-hearted mariners had melted his anger.

"Now come along, my boys! Get aboard quickly!" rang his orders. "Under way at once!"

Soon the air was full of sailors' belongings swinging to and fro from the end of the derrick.

Healthy, burly seamen sprang into the rigging with the alertness of trapeze artists. The deck of the *Pride of Wales* now presented animated scenes —gloom had been swept away.

As the tug took the strain, we slowly moved away. Shouts of "Happy Christmas" from the crowd were greeted with a salvo of snow balls in their midst, and much merriment ensued.

The strong N.E. wind lasted for days, and we had a glorious run down Channel. We passed a Portmadoc vessel at anchor off Harwich, the *John Evans*. She was weather-bound. They envied us going to the delectable Antilles.

Strange to say, with the exception of the Captain, second in command, and myself, no one in the ship had been south of Spain before. They had been trained in the hard school of the English coast, and to the apt pupil no better school existed.

On the way to the Bay, the crew settled down magnificently, and seemed more than happy. The afternoon watch below stayed on deck for the sheer joy of watching the *Pride of Wales* racing

K

along. Lighting their pipes, they took up a position clear of the spray. They would look with a delightfully cheery expression—an expression of real pride and satisfaction—at each sail in turn dragging at its creaking sheets. They were heading for the Tropics for the first time. To leave the hard sailing of the North Sea for sunnier climes was an event in their lives, and they were delighted with the prospects of losing sight of land for weeks at a time.

The new mate, too, was a great success. He had been in command of large sailing ships for years, but had retired. However, he happened to be strolling round the dock at Ipswich one day, and hearing that we were loading for the West Indies, expressed a desire to come with us, and would be quite happy to come as second in command. His services were gladly accepted.

The call of the sea rings constantly in the ears of a true sailor.

3

BOWS UP

In the dim light of Boxing Day morning, the Bay of Biscay frowned on us in no mistakable manner. It seemed to be going through a preliminary muscle-loosening exercise prior to taking the ring against us in real earnest. It was rolling up its sleeves.

A sudden change of wind to the opposite point of the compass confirmed our weather prognosis. The Captain had great experience of the Bay's terrible and merciless moods, and had reason to treat it with the utmost respect.

The new crew were early going through their baptism. Sails were taken in in rapid succession all the morning, and all hands were kept on deck that day. They were splendid in the rigging, and the Captain had rarely seen sails so well and neatly stowed, and as the gale increased so they seemed to temper up against it in a most confident manner.

The afternoon was spent driving additional wedges into tarpaulins covering the hatches, and securing the many coils of running gear of the sails not in use, and putting all deck movable objects in safe places. Snug under the fore top-mast stay-sail, the two lower top-sails, and the brailed-in-peak spanker, we entered the darkness of a night of disaster.

The idea of keeping so much canvas on was that we were not actually heaving to. She was kept full-and-by so that we were making a little headway in the right direction, and she was behaving splendidly, just the usual lumps of sea tumbling in through the fore-rigging. At the end of the dog watch the spanker was taken in and re-placed by the storm-mizzen stay-sail, reefed, and the watch went below, full of praise for the ship's behaviour. Taylor, a most experienced A.B., said she was the finest sea boat he had been in. Curiously enough, my grandfather, who commanded her during many years of her life, was emphatic on the same point. Her bows came up in a graceful flare, much like the bows of the famous Nova Scotia clippers, and as she plunged into a head sea she seemed to scatter it in an amazing way, whereas an old brig in which I sailed later used to drop her nose right under and pick up ten and twenty tons at a time. She would hurl it her whole length, and it would disappear in a cascade over the stern.

4

ON OUR BEAM ENDS

All went fairly well until the watch was called just before midnight. Ominous and violent rattling of the chain sheets of the two lower topsails foretold a sudden change of wind, and of all the unfortunate things to happen in a storm perhaps this is the worst. A wind-jammer, to remain under control, must of necessity follow the wind, which on this occasion had backed two points from northwest to west-north-west, but it was enough to bring us nearly broadside on to the sea.

The gigantic waves which she had been parrying so splendidly were now becoming masters of the situation. Perfectly helpless, we could sense a monster tearing towards our defenceless side, rising higher and higher, to crash into us, throwing the ship almost on her beam ends and completely filling the deck. It required little imagination, to those who heard the thud and felt the quivering timbers, to realise that something dreadful had happened.

The Captain and Mr. Peck, the Chief, were staggered and petrified; there was nothing that one could do, and more were rolling up. Between the tremendous blows that followed with monotonous regularity the three seamen, who had but a few minutes previously been called, appeared at the break of the poop. They brought the distressing news of the disaster they had seen as they crawled aft. The whole of the bulwarks on the port side from the fore-rigging to the quarter-deck had gone. Our brand-new lifeboat was a shattered shambles. The two water casks had gone over the side, the fo'c'sle had been filled to the level of the top bunks. What a home for those poor devils, and not a dry thing to put on!

The gaping rent in her side, measuring fifty feet, had been a blessing actually, for all the subsequent seas, finding no resistance, continued their wild rush in an uneventful manner, feeling satisfied that they had given that stout hull a pummelling *en passant*.

Not until daybreak did we find out the exact amount of damage; but the worst news of all was brought by the cook, who reported that the water in the big tank was all brackish and undrinkable. This meant that we had only a hundred and fifty gallons of water in the small emergency tank to last us for the rest of the passage, which turned out to be thirty-eight more days.

It appeared that when we were thrown on our beam ends, the large tank, which was nearly full and contained a thousand gallons, had moved slightly and strained the pipe that came through into the deck, with the disastrous result that salt water had been pouring in all night. Short rations of half-a-pint of water per day for thirst-quenching purposes and ablutions, and half-a-pint for coffee for breakfast and half-a-pint for tea in the evening, were all that we could look forward to, and a maximum of forty days given for the passage.

The day we arrived at Martinique we were on the last three inches of water in the small tank. We had no rain at all, and never sighted a sail or a ship all the way out. It is wonderful what human beings can become accustomed to and endure, and with quite good grace. Our daily dose of lime-juice helped matters along considerably by keeping our thirst quenched.

5

CARRYING ON

When we came out of the storm, which lasted five days, we were frozen and half starved, but eternally thankful. It was a big nuisance having no bulwarks, for the main-deck was like a half-tide rock even in fine weather during the remainder of the passage.

I could never understand why sailing ships that had suffered damage through stress of weather were rarely, if ever, taken to the nearest port to have matters put right. Here we were, at the beginning of a voyage, with our water supply reduced to a dangerous and most inconvenient minimum, and our comfort and safety materially interfered with, and yet with all the ports of Portugal, Gibraltar, and Madeira very little out of direct route. I do not suppose the thought of putting in anywhere ever entered our Skipper's head. "It would have to be put right at our port of destination," and we suffered accordingly throughout the long and tedious passage.

The strange thing was that the idea of carrying on with the passage, in whatever condition, was inculcated in the bones of all on board. The men never seemed to grumble or to expect any fuss that would make their lot the happier if bad luck stepped in. The shake-up in the Bay had confirmed the Captain's good opinion of the crew; they were just real hard-trained, good-natured British sailors who always came up smiling through all the trials and tribulations of the life.

The A.B.s—Taylor, Vagis, Grant, Richards, and the boatswain Palmer—came from Ipswich; they had spent their lives in collier brigs in the North Sea, and had roughed it all their lives. The cook went by the name of "Hokey," because during parts of the year he used to run a "hokey-pokey" barrow, and then, tiring, he would go to sea to pick up his health, as he used to say.

Although I sailed with many crews, these were, I think, the happiest. They had not come to sea against their will, nor with the intention of turning it into a penitentiary and counting the days when they would be free again. They came with a stock of good clothes and made the ship their home, their business centre and playground. They took a pride in their quarters, which were kept spotlessly clean. Each bunk was adorned with family photographs and trinkets. They made a good showing of their meagre meals, but much against their will they had to grow a beard owing to the scarcity of fresh water.

After the dingy and squalid dungeon of the old colliers, they thought the deck fo'c'sle of the *Pride of Wales* a real castle. Her clean decks, trim spars, and white sails made her look a queen in their minds when compared with the rusty and dirty appearance of the old *William Parker* (an ancient brigantine in which almost every sailor of the east coast had sailed). The tang of the deep and the eternal blue of the sea and sky seemed to promise them a paradise.

Good weather and southerly breezes took us well out into the heart of the ocean, away from the beaten track of south-bound ships. We were now following the course that Columbus and his ships steered on his first adventurous voyage, and we were bound for the same shores.

Almost three weeks to the day after leaving Ipswich, we picked up the trade wind. How delightful it seemed, with the cold blast of the Suffolk coast still fresh in our nostrils. The hardy mariners of the Dogger were much like children with a new toy. Sunday afternoon watch was too precious a time to waste in useless sleep, they thought. They would foregather on the fo'c'sle head, waiting and watching for unseen wonders of this great deep which was so strange to them. Quite suddenly we arrived in the realm that all sailors long to see and love to be in—that of the flying fish; it means good weather always, and a change of diet as well.

The silvery wings of the flying fish shimmering in the tropical sun, as they darted hither and thither in thick masses, gave us intense enjoyment. For three weeks we rolled leisurely through these entrancing avenues, escorted to-day by a flotilla of playful porpoises, to-morrow by hordes of gambolling dolphin.

6

HAPPY DAYS

I think some of the happiest days of my life at sea were spent on this voyage during the hours of the first night watch from eight to midnight. This duty came my way every other night. The

heat after a long day of relentless sun becomes
gradually tempered and one responds, both ment-
ally and physically, to the invigorating touch of
the cooler air and the refreshing dew. The old
ship, too, shows her approval. She springs suddenly from a lifeless indifference to a brisk stride.
Her ropes become as taut as the strings of a fiddle,
her canvas becomes crisp and she bends elegantly
to the breeze.

I was fortunate to be posted to the port watch,
which was Mr. Peck's. He was a type of man
that loved to have someone to talk to, and I fitted
in well with his ways. He was not only a highly-
qualified navigator, but also an accomplished
linguist, and always eager that others should share
his knowledge.

As we were bound for French islands, he gave
me lessons in French every other night. Resting
on the cabin skylight after our thousand paces up
and down the poop, he would become a French
Count and invite me to stay with him. A general
conversation about rooms, stairs, furniture and
pictures would be followed by a walk through the
grounds, kitchen gardens, and stables. Then we
would go into the town to do some shopping. He
would wish me to imagine that the ship was his
yacht cruising the Mediterranean. This was not
at all difficult during such delightful weather
under the glittering stars, and the graceful ship
brushing gently through a sea of phosphorescence
towards the enchanting Antilla. But the rub came
when I turned in at midnight, stabbed by pangs of
hunger, into a dark, rat-ridden bunk.

To vary the instruction, he would talk to me
about ocean navigation and its relation to astronomy.

I became engrossed in these new lessons. There was the night sky before us at its best and the friendly stars, which every sailor loves, became my absorption.

I was carried away by a desire to ask a star where we were on one of these wonderful nights, and this zeal brought great tribulation on my head. I may say that it is flagrantly against training and discipline for any budding officer to meddle even with the embroidery of navigation until he has waded for years through the drudgery of seamanship and mastered it. That night I found myself alone on the poop with the helmsman, and I decided to tiptoe below to get the Captain's sextant—without his permission.

I must have awakened him, however, for a few minutes later when I was deeply absorbed manipulating his magic sextant on a star and doing my Christopher Columbus stuff in good style, a ruthless hand came and separated me from it in no uncertain manner.

Many caustic words were spoken, including "Report to me at eight o'clock in the morning."

I slept but little on my watch below, wondering what yard-arm I would be hanging from in the morning. The sentence was ":to shoot the sun fifty times during the morning watch." Each observation had to be read off and noted accurately on paper. The criminal was the centre of much attention and curiosity during the punishment. Having finished well within time, I continued the imposition until I had reached sixty. This is where I went wrong again. One should never appear to enjoy a punishment on board a sailing ship. I was sent up aloft to grease down.

Here again I committed a grave seafaring offence. *I whistled.* Whistling was one of my besetting sins. On a wind-jammer it is inexcusable, as the offender is considered guilty of calling up the evil spirits of the storm. Most of the dirty jobs that could be found had passed through my hands before I was pronounced as cured of this habit. On this occasion, however, although I was high up on the fore-cross trees, the whistled strains of "Hob-y-deri-dando" filtered through to the deck. Every one stood aghast and gazed aloft with bulging eyes. I felt the air curdling around me. Unspeakable epithets rushed up the rigging. Even the ship below me seemed to squirm like a serpent. The sea was a boiling cauldron of shame. Dare I go below again? But the Captain demanded me to report instantly. I was in for it again.

There was one job I hadn't done, and it lasted until we sighted the islands. A disused condensed-milk tin was slung round my neck by means of a marline lanyard. It contained a viscous mixture of oils and fats. Armed with a quill, I had to lubricate the sheave and pin of every block from the truck to the deck on each of the three masts, and every block from the jib-boom end to the spanker-sheets.

It gave me great climbing confidence, and when we had to beat up to our anchorage and finally clew up all sails on arrival at Martinique, the good work I had done was much appreciated by the amused sailors. The ropes simply rattled over the lubricated sheaves.

7

THE SAILOR AND HIS FOOD

The well-trained sailor in those days was a strange type. He was so disciplined that he seemed bereft of initiative and of individuality. He seemed to know nothing but his job. He was never told the position of the ship from day to day, nor did he care where she was. He would be informed when she crossed the line; and he could guess when she was rounding the Horn or running through the Roaring Forties by the excessive discomfort of the going.

He was always kindly disposed towards a youngster who was being put through his pacings, but he rarely helped him to avoid trouble, because he thought it was part of the curriculum.

When a new crew joined, it was interesting to watch the settling-down process. The old shellback would proceed to impress his shipmates by selecting the best bunk, usually the top ones where the ports were. A short discussion on their respective length of service quickly appointed a "father," who took upon himself the onerous duty of keeping the house in order and order in the house. Almost every fo'c'sle, too, produced a sea-lawyer. He was a wag who took the line of least resistance, voluble of tongue and well versed in Board-of-Trade regulations. He would quote the law, chapter and verse, to his amiable and usually illiterate companions. He would prepare a case and mobilise his forces. They would march aft, hoping to get redress for a grievance, which was usually a question of food unfit for human consumption.

The memory of those pathetic processions of starved humanity will ever remain a blot on a great national service. The parade would be martialled at noon and marched aft in line ahead, led by the promoter carrying the unappetising junk on a tin, often guarded by a set of rough-looking doughboys. On those occasions the Captain's lot was not a.happy one. The men's sunken eyes and prominent cheekbones confirmed the honest purpose of this tragic errand.

What made the situation worse was that the remedy lay not in the Captain's hands. I have seen him remonstrating with as genuine a lot of men as ever sailed the sea. He appealingly invited them to compare the cabin's rations with their own any time they wished. He insisted that they should see what was on our table at that very moment.

I can visualise these splendid fellows now, trundling down the companion-way—caps in hand —their tanned faces rippling with amusement at the Captain's audacious invitation. We, too, tittered as they filed round our table. Our chunk of beef might have been an old friend lying in state, so sympathetically and reverently did they gaze upon it.

Passing the cabin door to regain the deck, their empty stomachs were set ablaze by a tot of rum which pleased them immensely. This was the spirit that nipped disturbances in the bud. After all, the expedition had been well worth while, they thought.

It is unbelievable that the barbaric conditions under which the deep-sea mariner carried on had existed from the Dark Ages almost to the end of the nineteenth century. In the early 'seventies public opinion was aroused by the persistence of one Samuel Plimsoll, a member of Parliament for Derby. He agitated by literature, by means of the Press and in the House, for legal protection for the splendid men of the Merchant Navy. He contended vigorously even to shaking his fists at the then Premier Disraeli that the time had come to put an end to the colossal loss of life that was going on in this important service. Men were being sent to sea in unseaworthy and overloaded ships which often had no chance of pulling through. Unscrupulous owners, however, benefited by these losses, for they had made sure on insuring these coffin ships, as they were known, for much more than their value.

By 1876 Samuel Plimsoll had won the day. An Act of Parliament, following an investigation by a Royal Commission, came to the rescue of our brave sailors. It was known as the Merchant Shipping Act. By its application the unseaworthy ships were caught and the overloaded betrayed.

By 1877 all British ships had their sides decorated by a small ring. So simple was the design and size that to the lay onlooker it would pass unnoticed, but to the seaman it conveyed a meaning of the deepest significance.

"Sammy," as the Hon. Member was affectionately called by sailors, became a god to worship. His name was acclaimed the length and breadth of the seven seas.

Jack, with his accustomed fullness of heart, let all civilisation know and realise his grateful appreciation of Samuel Plimsoll's untiring efforts on his behalf. He dubbed this precious and ever lustrous little "ring" the "Plimsoll Mark."

From a ship the nationality of which was in doubt passing on the high seas, Jack would turn his head

away and say: "She is not British anyway, no
Plimsoll Mark."

About the same period other drastic changes
affecting the safety and comfort of life at sea were
brought into operation by the arm of the law.
For the first time each ship had to carry specially-
designed lifeboats. Each person in the ship had
to be supplied with a life-belt. Life-buoys had to
be kept in convenient places for immediate use if
necessary. This was additional expense which
made the inhuman owner foam with wrath. He
was not yet finished with. Still another unspeakable scandal was exposed—the question of food.
In spite of good intentions of the Board of Trade
to improve the sailor's lot at the table, the unscrupulous owner was able to parry efforts in this
direction with fiendish cunning. This gave him
much sweet revenge. He was able to drive the
traditional coach and four through the Act. Finding
himself cornered and quite unable to cheat on
weight and measure, he romped home on quality
and recovered much of the leeway that he had
lost in profits by these costly reforms. Cheap and
poor quality of beef and pork was rushed into
casks of brine and sent to sea. Everything that
came into the ship's larder was the cheapest that
could be found. Yes, the owner scored freely now.

I add here a High Sea's dietary sheet for a week
in the *Pride of Wales*. All weeks and voyages were
the same.

MONDAY—

    Breakfast   Coffee.
                Hard ship's biscuits.
                Butter or marmalade.

Dinner Pea soup.
   Boiled salt pork.
   Biscuits and butter or marmalade.
Tea Milkless tea.
   Biscuits and marmalade or butter.
   Cracker hash (a baked pie made of crushed
    biscuits and small pieces of salt beef).

TUESDAY—

Breakfast As on Monday.
Dinner Boiled salt beef and doughboys.
   Plum-duff.
   Biscuits and butter or marmalade.
Tea As on Monday, but what remained of the
    pork would replace the cracker hash.

WEDNESDAY—

Breakfast
 etc. As on Monday.

THURSDAY—

Breakfast
 etc. As on Tuesday.

FRIDAY—

Breakfast
 etc. As on Monday.
Dinner Stock fish, boiled.
   Rice boiled.
   Biscuits with butter or marmalade.

SATURDAY—

Breakfast
 etc. As on Monday.

SUNDAY—

Breakfast As on Monday.
Dinner Boiled mutton tinned.
   Boiled rice with molasses.
   Biscuits and butter or marmalade.
Tea Cracker hash.
   Biscuits and butter or marmalade.

Ship's biscuits were the sailor's substitute for bread. I will later explain why the manufacture of bread was impracticable and impossible in those hard days of sail.

The biscuits were carried in large iron tanks, and for a short while at the beginning of each voyage they were fresh, crisp, and really quite appetising. But frequent visits had to be made to the tanks to replenish the lockers where biscuits were stored for immediate consumption. This allowed the brine-saturated air to make contact, and contamination followed. The freshness and crispness soon disappeared, and within a few weeks our staple food became mawkish and weevily. Breaking the biscuit into convenient portions for eating, these brown-headed little devils met one's gaze. To the first voyager it was a revolting sight. They were not a bit shy, they would just remain there and squirm. The old salt would take little heed—he would dislodge the tenants by gently tapping the biscuit on the table, and then go on with the meal. I soon had to get into this way or starve. Flour, too, suffered much the same fate in a sailing ship. After a few weeks at sea that delightful silkiness characteristic to the touch would depart, the nourishing gluten would die, and the contents of the bin would change into a granular powder. When it arrived at this stage it was useless for bread or cake-making. It even refused to respond to the energetic appeal of stiff doses of baking-powder. But it did mix with water to become a lifeless shape. This leaden mess would submit to many disguises. Rounded off into small balls it became doughboys. Bespeckled with stray currants it was plum-duff.

L

Served with and surrounded by molasses it was known as treacle-roll.

One rough day a doughboy escaped from my plate and rolled to the floor. It careered round the cabin bumping heavily into most things. When retrieved it was still intact—yes, they were tough things and most injurious to health. When plum-duff was about I used to probe to its depths for the currants. I relished those. Owing to water economy or laziness in the galley the currants were never prepared before they took part in the pudding. They could be seen resting in the centre of a dirty halo.

A word about Friday's fish. It was a desiccated and highly-salted variety of cod. It flew the Norwegian flag, and was the nearest approach to fossilisation. It easily defied the vagaries of weather in all parts of the world. Organisms feared it; sailors were made to eat it. Every Friday morning the cook would emerge from the galley armed with a powerful hammer and sheets of stock fish; each sheet was placed in a canvas bag. The windlass end on these occasions became an anvil, and here the cook would hammer the bag until he had reached a point of exhaustion. The fish would come out of the bag with its back broken. It was later made to dance for an hour in boiling water, and then sent to the table. Here it received the benediction in many languages of irate sailors.

Butter in the tropics became the consistency of machine oil. It was carried in 7-lb. hermetically-sealed tins. The day the tin was opened the butter had an agreeable odour and reminded one of dairy produce, but in the tropics it soon turned rancid and took sides with the other vile rubbish we had to eat. It was measured in cups or pannikins and applied to the biscuit with a spoon.

Sunday's mutton had a peculiar tang which searched disagreeably every corner of one's constitution. Although a change from the brine-sodden variety of meat, it was never popular. This, too, came to sea in hermetically-sealed tins. It was named by sailors "Harriet Lane." Harriet, it was understood, was a kindly body known to accommodate and befriend certain types of sailors. One day she disappeared, leaving no trace. In this form she came into Jack's mind every week.

Lime Juice, too, received prominence at this time. It figured in the Act. When a ship had been away from port ten days it became compulsory to issue a certain measure to every one on board. It was given as a preventative against scurvy. Anyone refusing to partake of his modicum was logged. That meant that he had committed an offence against the law. Deep-sea ships now were known as "Lime Juicers." I append two lines of a ditty:

Lime Juice and Vinegar, according to the Act;
There's nothing done in Lime Juice ships contrary
    to the Act.

Tea was my favourite meal of the three. During fine weather the cabin used to flourish a teapot which gave the feast a homely touch. Moreover, as I had a tuck locker, gooseberry jam made from fruit that I had helped to gather at one time or another went round with great relish. The meal was less enjoyable in bad weather; the tea was brought aft in a large iron kettle, a teapot required too much attention. Owing to a chemical agree-

ment going on between the tannin in the tea and
the iron of the kettle, the resulting infusion was
a vile and inky fluid. When sugar, nearly black
with molasses, was added, no characteristics of
tea could be traced.

The mention of gooseberry jam reminds me
of an episode which might have had serious consequences. During one of the voyages we had a
fellow on board who was unequalled for spinning
fantastic yarns about his life and experiences. No
one disputed the fact that he had led an extraordinary life and had committed extraordinary
deeds in that life, but how he had found time to
do it all in a forty-five years' span was the puzzle.
His general knowledge was astounding. He could
twist his tongue into seven languages. I liked him,
for his stories were told in dramatic and convincing
style. He got away with it by reason of being above
the head of his audience. One of his tall stories
concerned a drunken crew in a salt-petre ship off
the Horn. He claimed to have produced illicit
liquor by brandishing a magic wand, backed up
by a superhuman knowledge of organisms which he
had diligently collected and trained for the work.
During a night watch in the tropics I gave him a biscuit covered with the gooseberry jam. It used
to amuse me to see him tackle a biscuit. He had
but four teeth, two at the back on different sides
and two in the front which, fortunately for him,
were opposite each other and had to do all the
work. He reminded me of a rabbit feeding. He
instantly asked how much of the jam I possessed.
Could I spare him a 2-lb. jar? He would transform
it into a gallon of delicious wine which would be
ready in a fortnight—real strong wine. I was so

amazed at the man's audacity that I readily assented, although at the same time I wished my jam good-bye. He promised, if all went smoothly with the miracle, that the wine would be ready for my birth-day. He would creep every night down to the sail locker. He succeeded in working me up to a fever of excitement and expectation by bringing up a small bottle filled with a dirty-looking liquid. The cork in this bottle was tied down tightly with a rope-yarn. If in a week's time when the rope yarn would be cut the cork flew over the fore-yard, he said all would be well. If it failed then the spirits had failed him, and my jam would be wasted.

The jam actually was in a molasses jar, also buried amongst old sails. In this way a constant temperature was maintained. To it had been added water, and the whole was shaken vigorously every time an opportunity occurred to visit it. At long last the time had arrived to test the fidelity of his germs in the small bottle. We were rolling pleasantly amid a din of flapping sails. The fore-sail and mainsail hung in their clewgarnets waiting for a breeze. A full moon threw a path of golden sheen towards the Equator but a degree away northwards. From the fo'c'sle head where we had foregathered with the magic bottle, the dark form of the mate could be seen pacing the poop. Except for a slumbering "farmer" on the for'ard fife-rail, all was clear.

The little man, holding the bottle firmly in both hands with arms fully extended pointing towards the fore-yard, he commanded me to cut the rope-yarn and stand clear. I felt this practical joke had gone far enough. "Go on," he whispered insistently, "cut it." I gazed into his deep-set eyes—he looked intensely serious; but I was far from sharing his mood. I passed the blade of my sheath-knife sharply across the yarn. It was severed! In a flash a loud and ominous pop shot the cork high into the air. A creamy froth bubbled briskly over his tar-stained hands. "Yes!" he cried, "my friends are true to me, your birthday shall be a happy one, and I shall be drunk." I noticed the air was permeated with the aroma of yeast. I knew it well, for at home we used to knead our own bread. I asked him which of the planets had delivered it. It appeared that he had been foraging in the storeroom and had found half-a-dozen old potatoes, each not larger than a marble. They had been there since the ship was last in England. From these he had produced his yeast culture.

There was nothing now to prevent him from converting all the sugar, molasses, and marmalade in the ship into alcohol. My mind became much troubled. I had visions of a repetition of the incident in the salt-petre ship off the Horn, followed by mutiny, and all at my door. I longed to off-load my mind, yet I feared the consequences. My conscience, however, was pacified when the wine-merchant promised to destroy all traces of the dangerous experiment after the celebrations of my birthday. I did not enjoy the flavour of his wine; my gooseberry element had disappeared, but it was mighty potent, and made me ill. Much sugar had been added to help the jam along. Nor did I enjoy my birthday, for I was filled with apprehension as to the extent my shipmate would be affected by over-indulgence in his own product. When under the influence his small eyes would close but his tongue would waken to much volubility. I was able to secure the remains of the wine and the yeast bottle. I committed them to the deep for safe keeping.

When I finished my first spell at sea in 1893, these deplorable food conditions still persisted. Hunger, hardships, privations, and poverty were the keynote of the life. Within ten years the doom of the era of sail was certain. High banks of black smoke filled the distant horizon. Throbbing machinery encased in ugly bulks of iron profaned the realm that had been sacred to sail for a thousand years. The steamship had arrived!

8

VOLCANO

Forty-five days after leaving Harwich we were all excited. Both watches were ordered to keep a sharp lookout for land. The gathering power of the morning sun soon cleared a misty horizon, and we saw three interesting-looking tropical islands loom into view quite close by. They were Martinique, Dominica, and St. Lucia.

On the north point of Martinique was the great volcano, Mont Pelée, which seemed to fill the sky in that direction. On the other side at the foot of the volcano, we knew, stood the little town of St. Pierre, which later was to suffer a tragic fate, though as yet there was no sign of this. There was nought but our excitement at the landfall.

It is always very arresting to make a landfall like this. It seemed so uncanny, having travelled nearly four thousand miles without seeing a sight of land, that at an appointed hour it should stalk towards us out of the mist. It never failed.

The Captain gave the rocky spurs of the volcano that jutted irregularly into the sea a wide berth, with the result that the fast-running current between the two islands and the following wind brushed us quickly many miles to leeward.

We eventually opened up the town and found we had overshot it by many miles. This meant beating up to windward. Tacking ship every half-hour was most fatiguing on such a hot day, but we were amply rewarded for our labour.

With each tack this rugged island unfolded slowly its many beauties. The afternoon sun was now shining on those gaping gorges, giving a marvellous effect of contrasted light and shade. We saw the houses terraced on the lower slopes surrounded by trees. Huge rum and sugar factories hove in sight. For the last two miles our sails had been filled with a breeze laden with the peculiar and fascinating scent of rum, which the men thought was most tantalising. The rich aroma of molasses and the perfume of mellow fruit and spices filled our nostrils.

The nearer we got the more the breeze fell away, and the sea became like a millpond. Dozens of canoes paddled by negro boys swarmed to meet us, and the boys entertained us with their intrepid diving. One little fellow dived from the fore-yard arm, forty feet from the sea, swam under the ship and came up in a pool of blood the other side. He had unfortunately caught his back against a jagged strip of copper on the ship's keel and had badly lacerated it. However, two plugs of ship's tobacco soon made him smile.

At set of sun our day's toil was done and our passage safely over. We anchored in deep water only a hundred yards from the shore and right at the foot of the great volcano. As I looked up its rugged sides which towered four thousand feet into the sky, I was filled with wonderment. What a majestic sight! So steep was it that it seemed a link between the sea and heaven.

9

A BRETON BARQUE

Our first duty after anchoring was to sally forth in search of fresh water. For the last three days we had been drinking the dregs of the tank, a liquid rich enough in iron rust but intensely disagreeable. We made for the nearest ship, a French barque. The boat was manned by Mr. Peck, two A.B.s and myself. We were met by the Captain, a youngish man of smart appearance, and a very obliging person. While our water-casks were being filled, he invited the Chief and me to take wine with him. We were happy to do so. He served it out in tumblers, and so thirsty and exhausted were we, after our tiring day, that our glasses were refilled at frequent intervals.

Mr. Peck related in his best French the story of the mishap to the large water-tank. When at last we took leave of our kind host, we were surprised to find that our legs were unresponsive to our commands. Tacking behind Mr. Peck, I could see him lifting his feet so high that he might have been walking through a field of ripe corn. We scrambled into our boat, which was fortunately in the proper place to receive us. The two A.B.s, Richards and Grant, had been fêted as well. The Chief gave his rowing orders in French, as he found it difficult to get back into English. The men aboard were anxious for our return. They were eager for clean fresh water to quench a long-standing thirst. They rushed to the ship's rails as we bumped alongside in a most unseamanlike manner.

St. Pierre possessed no semblance of a harbour, and to see a couple of dozen sailing ships moored stern on, and within a few yards of the beach, was no uncommon sight. Here they loaded and unloaded their cargoes on a perfectly calm sea. Barges laden with merchandise filled in the spaces between the ships.

Next morning we had joined the line and were sandwiched between two Breton barques. The one on our port was the one we had visited, and whose Captain had been so kind to us. The friend-ship promised to develop.

Paul, the Captain, was still in his twenties, and with him sailed a cousin called Gaston. The ship belonged to their respective fathers, which ac-counted for Paul's early command. Gaston was doing a health cruise and, judging from his mode of living, he looked well on the way to destroy what little health he had. He put in a full day of gaiety and pleasure, and St. Pierre knew how to cater for the dissipated. There were wine, women, and dancing without measure. Paul aided and abetted his cousin in all his festive arrangements, and was always ready with the excuse that Gaston should be looked after.

For us, distractions came in rapid succession, so much so that the routine life of the ship became very dull, and it was very listlessly carried out. I was invited to a party on the French barque which brought me in touch with many rich French shippers and their families. The party was held on Sunday, and lasted most of the day. Paul was an excellent host. It was easy to see that he was a sailor more by force of circumstance than by any inherent desire. He never loitered in his ocean passages because of his anxiety to get to port. The call of revelry always rang in his ears. His cabin was large and well appointed for a small ship, and much taste was displayed in decorating it, particularly when in port. Silk curtains and puffed cushions were brought out of their hiding-places, and gay pictures of lovely women adorned the cabin panels.

The top of the officers' quarters formed a hybrid poop-deck. Here under an awning stretched over the spanker boom were deck-chairs and a table with a fascinating meal set on it. There was an extraordinary assortment of fruit, and many jugs of *vin ordinaire*. On the French ship this was carried in hogsheads and issued against scurvy, much like the English custom of issuing lime-juice. The wine was so plentiful that it was drunk in place of water for thirst-quenching purposes. One was always told it was harmless, but it had a way of getting into one's legs and into one's tongue.

The party went off in full swing. We danced to the music of François' accordion, supported by a banjo played by a pretty creole girl. The young women of the island, although not quite European looking, were very pretty, vivacious and attractive. The setting of the party as night drew on was perfect. The night temperature varies little from that of the day. The brightest moon shone over the shoulder of the darkling volcano. The twinkling lights of the town were reflected in the still depths of the sea close by.

Suddenly a rude fellow hurled himself across the fun and the romance. I thought at first he was a lunatic. He turned out to be a friend of Paul's, who had been invited to the party but had been unable to accept. He had heard, however, that his very pretty fiancée, Thérèse, had joined the party without his knowledge, and it seemed that he had now invaded the ship and demanded that she should be handed over to her true lover.

Paul knew that Thérèse was beguiling the time with Gaston in the 'tween-decks, and he thought it prudent for the time to keep the knowledge a close secret.

The angry lover, however, was not to be denied. He tore a hurricane lamp adrift from the rigging and commenced a search of the ship. Gaston, hearing the approaching storm, ran before it with his charge and came on deck for'ard. It was not necessary to tell him what to do.

The girl instantly leapt on a bollard, grabbed a running gear and swung herself on the top-gallant rail, slithered down a fender lanyard like a monkey, raced along the gunwhale of the lighter, plunged into the sea, swam ashore, ran like a stag along the beach and was soon safe. Gaston went the other way and sought refuge in the *Pride of Wales*.

The maddened lover seemed to have been temporarily quelled, but he diligently carried on with his search. No corner was left unsearched, and finally he met with a partial reward. Thérèse had found the 'tween-deck very warm and had discarded a flimsy wearing apparel—and her lover had found it. Getting no change out of Paul, he ignominiously retired over the ship side, with the treasured discovery tucked in his pocket.

Poor Thérèse. . . .

There was more fun later. An enterprising young couple had gone to sit out in the main-top, where they could get an unequalled view of the bay by moonlight and much peace. It was not a difficult place to reach via the lubber-hole, but not so easy to retire from, as most of the foot-holds had to be felt for. Don Juan, bold enough a lover, was no sailor, and instead of leading the way home he lowered the girl by her wrists through the lubber-hole. Finding no foot-hold she became frightened and began to scream. Some of us rushed to the rescue and found her hanging in as unenviable a position as a young lady would wish to be seen in. Her lower limbs kicked wildly in the air like the arms of a windmill. It was difficult to say where her dress was. The rescue work was amusing and easy, and it was carried out in the party spirit amid roars of laughter, in which the girl joined with gusto. Three of us climbed the futtock-shrouds; Paul and I each took a leg, the other fellow took the weight, and the lady was lowered to safety.

10

MARDI GRAS

We were fortunate in spending this time of the year in French islands. They were in their happiest mood. Like most Catholic countries, they enter body and soul into the pre-Lenten festivities. The

carnival spirit holds sway. Processions repre-
senting grotesque human beings and beasts mas-
queraded the town. Boisterous revelry works up
in a crescendo to culminate in a hectic madness
and irresponsible orgy on *Mardi Gras*. Paul,
Gaston, and I went ashore to join in the fun. Our
intention was to make for a café which was usually
conducted with much decorum. A little dancing
was thrown in to make it inviting. It had attractive
grounds, and one could see the bay through lines
of palm trees. Wine and food were served on the
terrace. To expedite our way through the town,
we chartered a vehicle with a strange quadruped
in the shafts, and a negro cocher half drunk on the
reins. We were soon in action. We were heavily
bombarded with ripe fruit. Then, having lost our
driver who was knocked off his seat by a juicy
but exacting melon, and finding our carriage un-
wontedly full of fruit pulp and sticky juice, we
decided to abandon ship and trust the rest of the
journey to our feet. The only way to make any
progress was to find a partner and dance our way
through. Every few yards a mellow missile filled
one's eyes with fruit essence. It was very good
fun. When we eventually arrived at the café, we
found it had lost a great deal of its respectability.
The dancing had become a bacchanalia. Decorum
had gone to the board. Wine and song and shouting prevailed. . . .

II

EXIT ST. PIERRE

Weighing anchor at break of day, we were off
for Guadeloupe, with the remainder of our cargo.

We little imagined, as we watched St. Pierre fading in the distance, the terrible fate that was awaiting it and its happy folk. In 1902 Mont Pelée, which the scientists had pronounced extinct, suddenly awoke from its slumber. Without warning, it burst forth into volcanic activity of immense fury and violence. St. Pierre and its surrounding country was whipped by maddened tongues of flame, followed by merciless showers of red-hot ashes, which soon completely buried the town. Those who tried to escape were caught by fierce gusts of poisonous gases. Rivers of molten lava rushed down the mountain side, destroying and killing everything in its way. Within fifteen minutes thirty-six thousand souls had perished, and St. Pierre ceased to be. Ships were burned to the water's edge. The sea around was a boiling cauldron. One vessel alone escaped, the English vessel *Roddam*, but her crew suffered terribly. One human being only was saved in the town— a negro who was in a cell in gaol waiting his hour of execution. He turned his freedom into a source of income, by appearing on the music-hall stage to give a graphic account of his miraculous escape.

We seemed to be paying visits to volcanoes on this voyage, for no sooner had Mont Pelée dipped out of sight than another appeared in the shape of La Soufrière. As we reached up for Point à Pitre on the port-tack, we came close to the rocky shores of Basse Terre, the lesser island of Guadeloupe. We then had a magnificent view of the volcano. It soared five thousand feet into the clouds. Visibility was particularly good. The huge ravines filled with luxuriant vegetation of every colour seemed almost under our jib-boom. Breaking irregularly at odd tangents, grey rocky boulders shot up to great heights, their crags and crevices trimmed with trees and their summit capped with green. Although La Soufrière had not been active for a hundred years, the island had suffered great damage from earth tremors from time to time. The islanders were always in a mood of expectancy in regard to them.

The run from Martinique had been most enjoyable. We passed over the spot where an important naval engagement had been fought at the end of the eighteenth century. It was between the English fleet under Admiral Rodney and the French fleet under Admiral de Grasse. The victory for England was decisive and settled the fate of the West India islands, most of which came under the British flag, and still remain. We had a great race with a small French steamer, which was carrying passengers between the islands. She found the *Pride of Wales* in a cheeky mood. We picked her up when doing the last leg to Point à Pitre. For an hour we plunged along neck and neck and very near together. Our courses and lower topsails were soaked with spray. As the breeze freshened, so we shot ahead, only to lose our lead again in the lulls. Approaching the port, the passengers were much interested to watch us taking in sails and running aloft to make them fast. They had none of that to do. We anchored early in the afternoon in the snug little rum-scented harbour, surrounded by sailing ships, all flying the tricolour of France.

12

A BUSMAN'S HOLIDAY

We found Point à Pitre in a very different mood from St. Pierre. The Lenten festivities were over, and the people were back in real earnest to the busy life of the island. France cannot boast of many possessions in these parts, but she gets every ounce out of Martinique and Guadeloupe. The islands in return are most loyal and responsive. Rum, sugar, molasses, cotton, tapioca, tobacco, and fruit are exported in large quantities and entirely in small sailing ships.

Grande-Terre, the larger island of the two, owing to its more adaptable contour is a seething forest of sugar canes. The greater portion of the sugar is converted into rum, and the large usines dotted here and there denote the extent of the business done in the commodity. Our letters of introduction from St. Pierre soon took effect. In the first week we much enjoyed a busman's holiday. The merchant who was taking our part cargo invited the Captain and myself to a cruise in his luxurious yacht. She was nearly as long as the *Pride of Wales*, but not so sturdy. The idea was to visit the small ports and the plantations of Grande-Terre. We were away two enjoyable days.

The yacht was a fore-and-aft rigged schooner, in which everything worked on travellers, which was most convenient. The only sail that was not so arranged was the jib. The owner's niece, a very charming and beautiful mulatto in the early twenties, was in command of the yacht, and she did her job well. This gave her uncle freedom to

M

entertain his friends, which afforded him as much pleasure as it did his guests. The delicacies of his table were of the non-stop variety.

Beating towards a headland to gain the open sea, we sailed through a great deal of congestion. There were ships and many reefs on the way. It was delightful to compare the devil-may-care and dashing seamanship of this girl with the stodgy, deliberate, and careful methods of the deep-sea man. Once we were petrified as she stood in for the nose of a sunken reef, came sharply into stays, and cleared the buoy by half a ship's length. One of the guests, a French skipper, immaculately turned out in a silk chemise and a spotless duck double-breaster, his white beard trimmed with symmetrical accuracy, had recourse to the brandy bottle to fortify his courage, remarking *Oh, là là! C'est extraordinaire, n'est ce pas?*

Going in to lunch, I was impressed by the lavishly-appointed cabin and a table such as a sailor seldom sees. We had no sooner sat down than there was a major disaster to the order and the trim of the feast. Losing the lee of the land, we suddenly plunged into a lively lop; two sharp gripes and most of the fine things on the table were in our lap. The remainder were on the floor mixed up with broken glasses and china. We had opened up a stiff breeze. Did the girl do it on purpose? I believe she did. Most of the guests thought the situation was amusing, but I had been looking forward to the good "tuck in" that so rarely came my way. We put about, and a fresh meal was served in smooth water. Sailors do not often do that kind of thing, and for me it was a very happy change from routine.

Pauline, our commander, was delightful. She had been to Europe, and spoke broken English with much fascination. Unable to find a word, she would coyly glance through the corner of her eyes, look skywards, pucker her brow, then, with an angel smile showing beautiful teeth, she would rapidly snap finger and thumb in an impulsive desire to charm the desired word to her lips. On the other hand she could deal with her crew with the ruthlessness of a Nova Scotia first mate . . . .

CHAPTER VIII

Sunshine in Florida

I

TO FLORIDA

ON our arrival at Point à Pitre, after a most pleasant interlude, we found our homeward-bound orders awaiting us. We were to proceed in ballast to Florida, the land of ease and orange groves, where at that time of year the rich Americans came in their thousands to get away from the rigours of winter, and to meet the sun.

The acutal sailing orders were vague enough: "Proceed to St. Petersburg, Tampa Bay, Florida, to load five hundred tons phosphate rock for Portsmouth, England." We could find no mention of this St. Petersburg in the usual Sailing Directions that mariners look to as a guide. A moderate-sized chart of Florida showed no channel or soundings that would be of the slightest assistance. We were to find a small jetty on the western shores of Tampa Bay. Along this jetty a small railway would bring open tipping-trucks rocking to the ship's side with our vile cargo.

The two-thousand mile run along the north Caribbean was our only crumb of comfort in the prospect. I was looking forward to this with great pleasure. The weather in the West Indies at this time of year is about as perfect as it can be anywhere on earth, and to enjoy it in a happy-go-lucky sailing ship in her best trim brings earth as near heaven as it is possible to do.

Two days before leaving, I was awakened in the early hours of the morning by the ship being jostled heavily, and it sounded as if pirates had taken charge of the deck. We rushed up to find many negroes running about, making fast a large lighter, which had brought our eighty tons of ballast. This ballast had the vilest stench imaginable. The buck nigger in charge assured us that the ballast was clean, harbour mud and fruit pulp stiffened with brick-bats, that it was quite harmless, and that in two or three days we should get used to it.

Mr. Peck, with handkerchief on nose, remonstrated with him in language fitting to the occasion, and wished to know if he was avenging the defeat of de Grasse on us in this cruel manner. We sailed away with three hatches off, much against regulations. Each hatch seemed to exhale its own particular kind of odour according to the different degree of decomposition going on in the hold. The buck nigger's forecast was, however, accurate; so much so that when we went high aloft into pure air we thought it was strangely sweet and even dangerously salubrious.

We noticed after a few days at sea that the haunts usually frequented by the ship's rats were deserted. It was quite agreeable to "turn in" and feel that a much-earned rest would not be disturbed by these unpleasant pests. The rats used to gnaw the timbers close to my ears, and race about in an unending procession round my head. It was discovered during one of the night watches that unusual liveliness was going on in the ship's hold. Here they had foregathered in hordes. They had found an atmosphere to their liking— a holiday resort; they could well imagine that they were back again in their native air, mid the filth of stagnant back-water and the mud of congested harbours. Old habitués of the fore peak had found a meeting place where they could exchange pleasantries, and flirt with their shipmates of the cabin. Here the blondes of the Baltic were serenaded by their dusky and demonstrative friends of the tropics. They turned the occasion into a veritable jamboree. They galloped in droves up and down this offensive heap, and giggled loudly. The Captain and I used to take up a position on the for'ard coamings of the main-hatch with a shotgun apiece. The setting sun shone towards the after part of the hold, and we could see them coming up in masses driven by the mate who used to rattle tins to start them off. Although we got much fun, we made little difference to their numbers.

It took three days to run down the length of the island of Cuba, and at times we were quite close in, and could hear the crack of rifle fire. The island then was in the throes of one of its many political revolutions. Rounding Cape San Antonio, we luffed under the weather shore. Mr. Peck, who had been to Havana, told me all about the tobacco industry of Cuba. It appears that the reason for the unvaried excellent quality of the Havana leaf is due to the fact that the mountain ranges here run latitudinally and regularly so. The result is that the sun plays on both the slopes of a ridge an equal amount, and the irrigation is likewise constant. I enjoyed these lectures on places and products as we passed them by. It was a series of geography lessons given under ideal conditions. We could see the mountain ranges quite plainly.

2

IN GOOD COMPANY

The sea in the Straits of Florida is notoriously rough. It is churned up into this roughness by the presence of many sunken rocks and fragmentary islands, and by a fast-running current flowing usually in the opposite direction to the wind. A light ship, however, makes light work of the worst conditions. But the experience was a warning that we were in for a rough time on our return passage loaded with phosphate rock.

Having picked up the low-lying land of Florida, we were soon at the entrance to Tampa Bay. Here a great surprise was in store for us. Anchored just inside the bay was a large portion of the American fleet. We thought it was probably there to watch events in Cuba. A fleet in those days looked formidable, with its impressive lofty hulls, high masts, many yards filled with sails, much deck hamper, bridges, and a smoking funnel into the bargain. It was obvious that there was no way in for us until some of the ships were moved. We notified by signal that we were bound for St. Petersburg. The Fleet suddenly became active. Many signals were flown, and it was interesting to see anchors being weighed, and a dozen men-o'-war steaming slowly to sea, passing on either side of us. We were then invited to sail in between the lines.

It was a wonderful and pretty picture to see this dainty little sailing ship, with her red ensign whisking the breeze, proudly sailing past these mighty ships, with her nose well in the air. We might have been carrying out an inspection. Each warship in turn gave us a friendly wave as we sped past under full sails. The *Pride of Wales* had two toy cannons on the poop muzzle pointing outboard. These did not go unnoticed, and caused much merriment in the naval eye.

Darkness caused us to anchor at the rear of the fleet, and we felt in good company. Tampa Bay that night looked as gay as Piccadilly. Port-holes and mast-heads flashed hundreds of twinkling lights. We could see in the distance the lights of Tampa City as well.

There were many sandbanks and divers channels between us and St. Petersburg, but there were no buoys to direct us. Tampa Bay, however, is non-tidal; so we were spared the nightmare of finding ourselves stuck on the edge of a bank on a falling tide.

It took us the whole day to sail eight miles; and this is how we did it. While the ship lay to a Kedge anchor, two boats were sent out as scouts, one towing the other which was filled with buoys made out of dunnage wood, a length of old rope and a fire bar. One of the American ships gave us a pinnace full of these precious materials, which are commonly used at sea burials too. The first boat took the soundings, while the other dropped the buoy. The boats remained at the last buoy about two miles from the ship. The *Pride of Wales* then slowly followed along the dotted line, frequently churning up the sand as she went along. Four of us only were left on board to do the sailing and anchor-tripping.

At the end of this perfect day the anchor was dropped. A large hotel and a home-made pier had been located in the dim distance. During the night the wind shifted, with the result that the ship got stuck on a shoal. Break of day brought much excitement. We were surrounded by boats filled with negroes, who provided us with fish and oysters, which all hands very much enjoyed. A dozen boats made fast to our jib-boom and tugged us off the shoal, and towed us in grand style to our journey's end. Remembering that our objectionable ballast had to be dumped, we anchored a quarter of a mile from the pier. The Captain, with much consideration for his crew, engaged a dozen negroes to get on with this work, and, before the day was out, the ship was sweet and clean once more.

Many fashionably-dressed people from the large Hotel Detroit flocked to the pier to see this strange craft that had arrived at their door. They had not seen an English sailing ship there before. In the light of the moon and with the aid of a few fore-and-aft sails, we glided gently to our position alongside the small jetty. A quaint trip was over.

3

PAIN AND A MULE

For the last three days before berthing I had been tortured with the agony of toothache. One eye was completely closed and even my mouth was partly closed on account of my swollen face. My tongue, too, was skinned by the applications of pure chloroform to the unruly tooth. A negro told me there was a coloured fellow working on a plantation seven miles away who could draw teeth quite well. If I were to get up at six o'clock the next day, he knew of a pack-mule going that way, and he would arrange for my passage. However, there was no need to get up at six, for I had paced the deck all night in pain. As soon as the sun showed its head above the bay, my negro friend came down the pier to meet me. The old mule was waiting with a heavy pack covering him well up. A negro boy and I finished the load, and off we went in search of this hewer of wood and drawer of teeth. From that moment until my return to the ship eighteen hours later, I have no hesitation in saying that was the most varied and extraordinary day.

Within a few moments we were wending our way along a bridle path through a maze of matted undergrowth, the famed everglades of Florida. We were covered and surrounded by a jungle so thick that neither sun nor sky was visible. Weird and strange noises on the right and on the left often made me wonder what would spring upon us from the unknown tangle. Squawking and squalling forest rodents raced along the intertwined branches overhead. The roar of alligators and the song of strange birds mingled discordantly with the clatter of the rattle-snake, "*Keep yo legs well up, Sah, dis am bad place*," was the frequent advice of my youthful guide. The strength of the morning sun made the conditions humid and sweltering. Deprived of the luxury of a saddle, my lower half was soon competing with my face for pain and discomfort. Disagreeable wafts arose also from our pathetic mule, which invited hordes of pestilential flies to join us as escort to complete the malaise.

Stopping at a brook to water our steed, we were surrounded by a pandemonium of rattles. The sun was shining on a parched piece of ground. Here a knotted confusion of rattle-snakes, like a huge mat, were basking happily. Their tails waved a warning that they would resent interference. My companion hurled a tin from the pack into the middle of them. They swiftly disentangled and slithered nervously into the undergrowth. The sharp edge of the missile had wounded a large snake. We dismounted and finished it off. Placing it over the hilt of my sheath-knife, I carried it aboard and it became one of my cherished curios.

A magic thing happened at this point—my toothache vanished. Having made two or three calls at negro cabins to discharge part cargo, we finished our tiring journey in open country, having passed on either side miles of fragrant orange groves.

The dentist was a kindly-natured, grey-haired negro, and he welcomed me to his cabin. I said good-bye to my driving companions of the jungle, for they were not returning that day. The duel with my new friend the dentist was terrific. We fought furiously, and after I had been dragged round the room at the end of a dirty forceps, the tooth and a large piece of my gum were proudly brandished before my eyes. He told me he did not get much practice, and he apologised for the mess I was in. I was bespattered with blood.

My journey back was both amusing and irritating. The dentist had a neighbour who owned a donkey that was wont to go riderless to St. Petersburg to collect stores. He took his own time, which was usually the best part of the day. All I had to do was to sit on his back and bide his time. He would feed, drink, and loiter *en route* as he pleased. The pace, now that I was better, did not suit me. I dismounted and went into the thicket to cut a cane with which I intended to urge my steed on; but I did not get the chance. When I returned to the path the donkey would have nothing to do with me, and he showed his disgust by performing wonderful acrobatic feats with his hind legs, narrowly missing my face. So I decided to continue the journey under my own power. Making a detour to pass my friend, he waved me a fond farewell with a spectacular effort.

Passing through an avenue, I heard some one whistling a popular English air. I stopped. I could see a man some distance away working among the orange trees. He responded to my call. I asked him if he was English. At first he suspected me, but he soon unbent, and when he found I was a sailor he invited me to his cabin to tell him all about myself. We had coffee and cakes, the while three little piccaninnies gazed into my distorted features, half afraid of me. My host was an Englishman, the son of titled parents. He had found a career in the navy ill-suited to his roving disposition and, seizing an opportunity, he cast off his garb of blue and gold to don the tatters of the road. After a four-thousand-mile trek, labouring a day here, navvying a day there, varying his form of travel in accordance with the dictates of his errant mind and the state of his finances, he eventually reached Florida, and took such a liking to growing oranges in the attractive climate that he settled down there, little thinking that the *Pride of Wales* would one day anchor five miles from his door and that I should pop in and see him. I believe I had extracted information from him that he had denied to others, for he was anxious that our meeting should only be discussed on broad lines.

Darkness suddenly came, and caught me with the most difficult part of my journey to do. Once in a jungle there is nothing to be seen to give a sense of direction, and to be lost in such a place fills the heart with utter despair. Criss-crossing tracks of humans and beasts seemed to favour perplexity and to lead to no home for me. As I was sparsely clad in an open-fronted twill shirt and a pair of blue serge slacks, the damp air of the night caused my teeth to chatter. I caught a glimpse of a faint moon and, remembering its bearing the previous night, I changed my course. The new ground, however, suddenly became soft. I sank into it at each step over my ankles. The hum of mosquitoes became louder. Turning to extricate my slowly-sinking legs, I fell. I gave a fierce yell. Groping aimlessly, I found a root of a tree and pulled myself clear to hard ground. My piercing shriek had been heard, for a welcome light came to a window quite near. A woman's voice with a very strong American accent asked what was the matter. I shouted, " I am a young sailor from a British ship at St. Petersburg. I have lost my way. Do please help me."

The tall form of a woman carrying a lamp slowly approached. She said: " Stay where you are till I get to you. You are in a bad place."

Within five minutes, an attractive American girl of sixteen was introducing me to her mother, who was an invalid. Their wooden shack, built on stilts, was only half a mile from the *Pride of Wales*. They made a great fuss of me, and administered to my needs. In my anguish I had scrunched the lacerated gum and set it bleeding again, and my face was covered with blood and mud.

At midnight, Margaret and I, carrying a candle lamp, were strolling happily arm in arm towards the pier. The Captain had been anxious about me, and had not been able to sleep. When he saw me covered with caked mud and blood, and a rattle-snake suspended from my belt, he was much amused, and only wished that my mother could have seen me then.

4

A HOLIDAY

The following Sunday was an interesting day, during which we watched a unique competition. About fifty negroes, all men, sat in a semi-circle round the end of the pier. Each was served with a basket containing so many dozens of oysters. Over each pair stood a scrutineer; all hands of our ship were asked to officiate as such. At the sound of the ship's bell they were off; the one who opened and consumed the greatest number of oysters in a given time was adjudged the winner. It was incredible how slick they all were. Each oyster had to be consumed as it was opened, and it was remarkable how each head went back for a long time with the regularity of soldiers carrying out a drill. The winner was dubbed Oyster King of the season. On this occasion he had consumed just over six dozen in fifteen minutes.

As there was no sign of our cargo arriving, the ship was crowded with visitors. The rich Americans and their families from the Hotel loved to spend the whole day sitting about the deck, smoking and reading, and thoroughly enjoying the atmosphere that a sailing ship provided. They suggested that a tea-party on board would be very popular. The Captain was delighted with the idea. The chef and an able staff were soon on board from the Hotel. The old ship's main-deck was transformed into a fashionable restaurant. It was a fascinating mixture of land and sea life. There was the lavishly-laid table, decorated with flowers, rich-looking cakes and plated teapots—and it was all surrounded by belaying pins, ropes, spars and sails and the smell of tar.

We had a glorious day for the function, but a brisk breeze blew the ship in jerks against the jetty. There was a danger of doing damage to the flimsy structure, so we cast adrift and swung to the anchor a good distance from the pier. This gave a finishing touch of realism to a novel afternoon. The ship, being empty, heeled over delicately as each gust whistled through the rigging.

5

A VISIT TO ORANGE GROVES

Florida's ideal climate is to a great extent responsible for the production of probably the most luscious and best-flavoured oranges in the world. An extraordinary amount of pain is taken by the growers, each plant being diligently and regularly looked after —no mother could look after her child more.

Occasionally frosts visit the State, under cover of darkness; and when we were there an inch of snow fell one night. Of course this is enough to ruin every tree. Exacting measures are therefore taken to protect the groves against these sudden visitations. Log fires are laid in readiness at regular and frequent intervals between the orange trees. A night watchman is always on duty. Should he give the alarm, plantation workers rush out and light the fires. Within a short time the countryside is all aglow. Orange groves are transformed into a fairyland of crackling fires, and the air around is charged with a delicious and aromatic perfume as the embers burn. Soon a stratum of gentle heat settles above the delicate trees and shields them from harm. The snow is transformed into re-freshing rain, and the frost driven away.

6

DESERTERS

St. Petersburg in those days existed only in name. All that could be seen from the bay were a few wooden huts on stilts dotted here and there on the edge of a small wilderness, in addition to the Hotel Detroit. To-day it is a large and fashionable resort with a population of fifty-thousand and a hundred hotels. Quite close, on the other side of the peninsula facing the Atlantic, is the famous resort Miami, with its incomparable beaches where high life and wanton pleasures fill the day. I should imagine St. Petersburg to be a sedate overflow of Miami. The calm bay affords many miles of safe sailing and boating; and to the man

FACE PAGE 192

Sugar Loaf, Rio de Janeiro

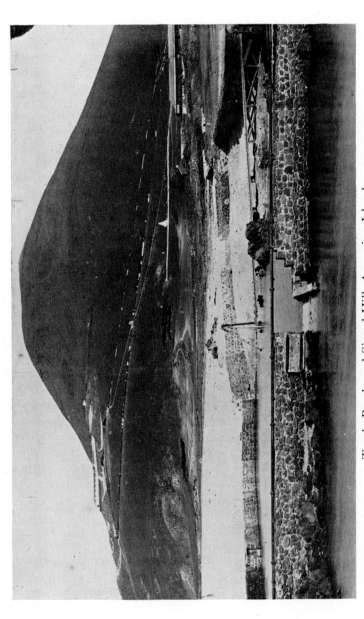

Turtle Ponds and Signal Hill, Ascension Island

Coal was carried here from Cardiff in *Pride of Wales*

who loves fishing, his heaven lies outside his window.

On one occasion fresh meat rations from the small store had not arrived. Probably there was none for anyone that day. The cook, on reporting the fact, was sent out on the bowsprit shrouds with a fishing line. In half an hour he had caught enough fish to feed ten hungry sailors, and the assortment would have baffled the selective genius of an epicure. Among them was a puffer fish, which if tickled round the gills would swell until he looked exactly like a football—he would deflate as well with a peculiar hissing sound escaping from his gills. The negroes on the pier fished for only one particular kind of fish, all others being thrown back into the sea.

Our faithful friends from the hotel were thrilled and much entertained for three days with an interesting phase of ship life. To them a sailing ship was as refreshing as a good play. Most of them came from States a thousand miles away from a seafaring atmosphere. The yards were being stripped of the gossamer sails of the tropics, and in their place the sturdy canvas of heavy weather was being bent. To the frivolous onlooker it was amusing, but to us the change had a deeper significance. We were preparing once more for the fierce fights of the Western ocean.

A.B.s Grant, Richards, and I were working together on the fore lower-topsail yard, quietly securing to the jack-stay with new marline that tough storm-sail. It was a perfect day, and as we glanced round those peaceful surroundings and the tranquil bay it put us in a mood quite out of sympathy with our work.

N

Grant, never over-communicative, suddenly burst forth into a tirade of deep reasoning on these lines: Why should we go on a small sailing ship, deeply laden with phosphate rock, with bad food, little sleep, wet beds, wet clothes, frozen extremities, fighting gales, pelted by gigantic seas, continuous work and poor pay, when we can stay in this paradise with fish and oysters for nothing, chickens and pigs running wild, delicious fruit and plenty falling in one's lap? What an ideal spot to desert at! . . .

I went ashore that night to dine with Margaret and her mother; and, returning, met two men on the pier walking briskly in the opposite direction. I recognised them to be Richards and Grant. I wished them good night. I should have said good-bye, for that was the last seen of them as members of the crew of the *Pride of Wales*. Bending storm-sails in sunny Florida had opened their eyes.

The disappearance of these two fine young seamen was a tragedy the full gravity of which was not realised until we reached the wilds of the ocean. Exhaustive efforts were made to replace them, but without success. No sailor wanted to leave those ports in a small wind-jammer, even at inviting rates of pay. The little place was set throbbing with excitement when the news spread that two of our seamen had escaped. People from the Hotel, mounted on horses, organised themselves into groups, and, with the aid of negroes acting as beaters, they systematically worked a large area of rough country and everglades, besides visiting most of the orange groves around. They had all subscribed to a pool, and the finders of Grant and Richards would obtain a substantial amount, on

the condition, however, that they should entertain
the rest to dinner and relate their story from
behind champagne bottles.

I knew Richards fairly well. He was a deep
thinker and a great reader, and if his thoughts
were fashioned on his style of literature, he would
be difficult to track down. And Grant would make
an obedient follower. They apparently had secured
a new rig, for all their kit was accounted for,
and it had been neatly stowed away.

7

GOOD-BYE, ST. PETERSBURG

Most vessels habitually carrying phosphate rock
were fitted with a platform which had the effect
of lifting the cargo and so raising the vessel's centre
of gravity. This in turn diminished the labouring
and straining when in a turbulent sea. The sailing
was also much more comfortable for the ship's
company. Wood being cheap, we set to to build one
for the occasion. Old beef casks came in useful
as foundations. The finished product pleased the
designers, the Captain, and Mr. Peck. The full
cargo ran the whole length of the ship now, thus
evenly distributing the weight. It looked like a
miniature mountain range instead of the usual
mountain amidships which was so injurious to a
wooden ship.

In view of the fact that we would in all pro-
bability be crossing the Atlantic two hands short,
the Captain very rightly and wisely refused to take
more than four hundred and seventy tons, which
meant that the owner would lose £50 in freight,

but he was saving an equal amount in pay. With the lower rim of the Plimsoll ring just awash, I must say the *Pride of Wales* looked in capital trim. She lay for two days to her anchor just clear of the pier. Crowded pleasure craft now from all parts of the bay leisurely cruised around absorbed in admiration, and it would be difficult to find any sailing ship that could play the part of a pretty model to better effect, for although advancing in years her beautiful lines remained unimpaired. The white-tipped yards covered with tightly-furled tough canvas, trimmed to the breeze, gave her an alert and sprightly air.

The day before we sailed, the Captain, Mr. Peck, and myself were invited to the Hotel to a farewell dinner. It was a memorable feast interspersed with touching speeches and ocean melodies. Our stay at this little spot had been most pleasant, full of charming episodes, acts of hospitality and friendship. And now they had come to an end. We carried away with us memories of happiness and gratitude that time would never erase . . . Good-bye, St. Petersburg. . . .

8

EXCITEMENTS

Our departure at ten next morning was not free from a touch of drama. With topsail, jibs, and staysail set, and with the last shackle on the windlass, ten minutes later we would have been slowly gathering way and heading for the gulf. From the midst of well-wishers gathered at the head of the jetty a clear voice rang out, calling the Captain to

go ashore again. It appeared that a destitute
Englishman had arrived at the pier in a most
pitiful and distressed condition. Hearing that a
sailing ship was bound for England, he set out to
tramp many miles along the hot, dusty, and hard
roads in the hope that he could make the passage
home to see his very old mother before she died.
Surrounded by well-to-do people, he looked a
tragic figure—bootless, coatless, penniless and
hungry, his naked feet a gory sight, sobbing like
a child, for although a hefty fellow it was easy to
gather that he had been up against it, so to speak.
He entreated the Captain to give him a chance to
prove his worth and work his passage home. The
Captain, warning him that he would not find an
ocean crossing in the *Pride of Wales* a joy ride,
nodded his kindly assent; and as this stranded
Briton took his place in the bow of the boat, now
smiling happily, he received a farewell cheer that
should ring in his ears all his life.

This big kindly-natured fellow, knowing little
about the sea and less about a sailing ship, soon
worked himself into the hearts of all on board.
His pluck in suffering, his utter disregard for danger,
his insistent desire to share all the gruelling hardships of our life, knew no bounds. He made us
feel proud that we had taken compassion on a soul
who, through no fault of his own, had been shunned
and neglected throughout his unfortunate life.
Inheriting the kit left by the deserters, he looked
odd with nothing quite buttoning up and fitting.
Most unfortunate of all, the two pairs of sea boots
were useless, with the result that his legs and
feet were always wet and often frozen from Key
West to the English Channel. Even this failed to

discourage him. He used to say, "Ah, I have a nice warm bunk waiting for me." He had been given the one abutting the galley, which really was cosy in the winter, but unbearable in hot weather.

When we gained the open sea, it was unmistakable the happy mood the novel distribution of the cargo had put the ship in. She seemed to be tripping on tiptoe from wave to wave, and her roll was gentle and even. The inventors had every reason to be pleased with their work, and they chuckled merrily.

Much like our experience in the French yacht at Guadaloupe when she threw our lunch off the table, so the *Pride of Wales* entering suddenly into angry, broken water, off The Keys of Florida took half a dozen deep and sudden plunges. It was blowing fresh. The royals, flying-jib, and gaff-topsail had not been set. To our horror we heard a rumbling noise much like distant thunder, followed instantly by a loud crash that was terrifying. The coastline round the south-western and southern end of Florida is a confused mass of detached rocks and small islands, and the sea is vicious. Had we struck a sunken rock? No, for we were sailing gaily on, but the previous pleasant movement had gone. The ship had suddenly become fidgety and fretty. "My God!" the Captain exclaimed, "the platform has collapsed." So it had, and about three hundred tons of rock had fallen nearly five feet into the bottom of the hold. A ship that could stand that sort of treatment must necessarily be strong. Was she at that age equal to the blow? We rushed to the pumps to seek the answer. After a dozen whisks at the fly wheels, our faces lit up with joy. All was well. We turned back into smooth water to check her trim in case the cargo had shifted to leeward. We found that it had, and we spent the rest of the day throwing chunks of rock about, which made our hands bleed. The weight distribution was now all wrong, as the whole of the cargo was below the level of the sea. This was not too pleasant a thought when we reflected that the stormy Forties were between us and home.

A second thrill came our way when we were a hundred miles north of the Bahamas. This brought us to the verge of disaster. It was just before nightfall. Scudding along before a fresh breeze under a good pressure of canvas, we hit an obstacle several sharp blows. Right alongside, under our lee, was a huge raft of heavy balks chained together. It seemed to be forty feet long and about thirty feet wide. Most fortunately for us we had grazed along its side, although the first blow had chafed the prow without doing any harm. Had we hit it full on, we must have gone down like a stone. One poor ship had apparently just gone to its doom, for we ran into wreckage a minute or two later. Moreover, we had noticed splintered marks on the raft at the point of impact. On the one end it had a chain bridle, which led us to conclude that it was in tow at one time and had broken away from the tug in a storm.

Of the many distressing mind-tortures that afflicted relatives of sailors in the old days of sail, none was more harrowing and heart-rending than the long wait for news of a missing ship. What had been her fate, and how had the end come? Taking the case of this raft, one must remember that the danger lurks stealthily between the waves. It creates no visible commotion. It is most difficult to detect in daylight except under favourable surface conditions. It is impossible to detect it at night. It haunts a trade route for long periods. Driven hither and thither by the storm, it visits wide areas in its deadly mission. Its victims are unknown and uncounted.

Our passage across the Atlantic took forty-one days. We encountered many dirty patches of short duration and one terrific storm which lasted four days. This we met in the usual stormy zone. Being sadly undermanned, the few of us left suffered great privations. Every time we stayed ship or shortened canvas meant keeping the below watch on deck and the pumps had to be kept going every hour.

I have every reason to remember the third day of the storm. It was the first time that I was sent aloft under such conditions. I had seen the ship below me from all parts of the masts in fine weather. I had enjoyed gazing round the limitless sea from the giddy tips of the yards, but when the tempest howls its defiance a bird's eye view of the same ship wrestling and struggling against this maddened savagery turns the mind into a fire of fear.

The weather clew of the furled fore upper-topsail was shaking loose and had to be made secure. Taylor and I were told off for the job. Taking off our oilskins, coats, and sou'westers, we were told to stand by under the lee of the fo'c'sle until Mr. Peck, who had taken the wheel, gave us the signal—GO. I can see Taylor now, bare-headed, with a good stock of dishevelled hair, a rough beard through which flowed copious rivers of tobacco juice; his keen deep-set blue eyes peeping through heavy lashes, looked anxious. A large red handkerchief with white spots circled his neck, and the ends of the scarf were tucked into his blue jersey. Although there were intervals of several seconds between the onslaught of each great wave, we had to be pretty nippy to get high enough up the rigging to be out of harm's way, for this part of the ship receives all the punishment and is a veritable danger spot. We were off!

For the moment our two lives were in Mr. Peck's hands. The ship was gliding down into a trough which looked like a mammoth grave. We were over the sheer poles like two monkeys, our heavy sea-boots clattering on the wooden battens as we raced towards the futtock-shrouds. When we reached the upper-topsail yard, Taylor lashed one end of a spare gasket round my body. While he was doing this I chanced to look below, and saw a sight which made me shudder.

The shape of the *Pride of Wales* looking from aloft always reminded me of a coffin, broad at the shoulders and tapering towards both ends. On this occasion, with her decks white with foam from the swirling and seething seas, she looked like some ocean giant lying in state. Slithering on to the foot-rope and keeping close together, we carefully crept out. Then we were exposed to the full force of the gale. The ship lifted high her little bow in a desperate effort to avoid the blow of a heavy sea. The yard assumed a steeper angle. I started slipping away, and I felt nothing could save me, for my body was being blown away from the yard. Taylor, straddling a stirrup, tautened the life-rope, and pulled me towards him. I could feel my blood freezing and my face

turning into stone. I yelled at Taylor to ask him
if he thought I could stick it, but the shriek of the
wind, the whistling ropes, and the deafening noise
of the breaking seas muffled a mere human voice.

Gazing vacantly at a bleak and angry horizon,
looking down for the first time on a great wilderness of terror and torture, I was seized with despair.
Not a soul or a sail in sight, the world seemed
deserted. There was only this tiny ship and its
nine miserable hungry occupants conjuring with
the wrath of God.

Taylor had got to grips with the sail. He
passed my soul and body lashing through a becket
on the jack-stay and then tied it round his own body.
This secured both of us and helped to restore my
confidence. In order to make a good job of the
sail we had to unfurl half of it. In a flash another
demon had arraigned itself against us. Bellying
high like a balloon with each weather roll, the
sail threatened to beat us backwards off the yard.
We now fought like tigers in an effort to keep it
smothered, but so violent were the convulsions
each time the storm got control of it that time and
time again we were forced to let go or be cata-
pulted over the yard. During one of the mauls
Taylor was struck in the face by the heavy reef
cringle—he rocked to and fro like a drunkard,
apparently stunned. His nose bled profusely.
I was reminded of this when his warm blood,
blown by the gale, caught my face. So tightly
did we grip the tough canvas that every time
the sail beat us clear it tore our nails away from
the quick.

Returning to the mast, my finger-tips bleeding
and forehead bathed in perspiration, I clasped it

like a frightened child its mother, and thanked
God that another lesson in seamanship was over.
It was quite within the bounds of possibility that
such a job could come one's way in the depth of
night. What then? These small ships were hard
schools of the sea.

9

JEFF

Jeff, our worthy passenger, was by this time in
a sad state. When he joined us, his constitution,
though he possessed a powerful frame, bore traces
of a hazardous existence. A life of vagrancy, mal-
nutrition, and neglect had brought him down to
a low ebb of vitality. Sea-sickness, starvation, and
exposure quickly reduced him to a physical wreck.
Great boils broke out all over the lower part of
his body. Unable to sit, rest, or sleep, he became
a subject of pity and sympathy with us all. So
long as the weather allowed it, we were able to
alleviate his suffering by applying hot fomenta-
tions. We had fourteen pounds of linseed meal
in the medicine chest, but it had gone maggoty.
Powdered ship's biscuits were used for poultices
until his condition became worse and prohibited
such extravagance. The advent of stormy weather
put an end to what attentions we could give him.
Full of consideartion for others, he left the fo'c'sle
and made the sail locker his abode so as not to
disturb the sleep of his shipmates. He used to
roam about the deck day and night wet through,
doubled up in pain, but he seemed ever to be on
the spot to lend a hand to either watch when there
was a job of work to do. When the great storm

came he was brought aft to the lazaret. Here, owing to the lack of head room, he crept about like a beast on all fours, sometimes dozing on his knees, wedged in a corner with the side of his face on the floor.

The day Taylor and I were struggling up aloft, Jeff heard Mr. Peck cursing and blinding, as he and the cook were setting the mizzen stay-sail just above him. He crawled up to lend a hand, and afterwards went with them along the main deck where conditions were deplorable for a sick man. They adjusted the foretop-sail braces which made our job aloft the easier. Here a calamity befell Jeff which turned out to be a blessing in disguise. The ship's deck was flooded by a heavy sea. Mr. Peck and the cook were able to jump on the fife-rail to save themselves. They thought Jeff was off for his last journey. He was soon swallowed up by the rushing torrent. He collided heavily with the after-capstan, to end up in the lee scuppers, half drowned. A miraculous operation had, in that instant, been performed. The force of the collision had dispersed two of the larger abscesses. He was picked up and dragged to the lazaret, unconscious and a gory mess.

When Taylor and I returned to the deck, we rather expected a hero's reception, but not a soul could be seen anywhere. Calling at the galley for our oilskins, we found it empty with evidence of much disorder. The stove was white with brine and the fire black out. Coming aft, we could see the wheel lashed as before, and the mizzen stay-sail blown to bits. From the booby-hatch of the lazaret came the cook hurrying to the cabin for brandy. He told us that Jeff was

passing out. I gave a morbid look down the hatch.
I could see the Captain and Mr. Peck busily engaged in emptying him of salt water and massaging
the region of his heart. His head was lying in a
pool of blood which was pouring from a deep
lacerated wound on his temple. Symptoms of
cyanosis and exhaustion were much in evidence,
but artificial respiration and massage worked wonders, and at last Jeff's eyes half opened. Seeing
the Captain and Mr. Peck above him, he gave an
appreciative smile.

The next day, coming on deck at noon, I saw the
Captain at the wheel, a most unusual place to
find him. It appeared that the boatswain and his
two companions of the watch had been sent to
trim the main-braces. They were having a rough
time in the lee-scuppers with the sea rushing
up to their shoulders. Their curses were heard
by Jeff who was close by in the lazaret. The next
moment he had crawled on deck, and was soon
tailing on their rope. He said he was happier
moving about. So in this way Jeff limped into
convalescence, swathed in bandages and reeking
of iodoform. Jeff possessed a stout heart.

10

TEN POUNDS REWARD

The presence of many gulls heralded our approach
to land. Early on the 5th of May we ran into
soundings. Our dead-reckoning position placed
us fifty miles south-west of the Scillies. The wind
was N.N.E. It was bitterly cold, with sleet showers.
The look-out reported a small boat ahead under·

a lug sail, and a small mizzen, too, was set. A
man standing up in the bow was waving his cap
to draw our attention. We came shaking into the
wind and backed the main yards. What was the
matter? We wondered why such a small craft
should be so far out. Presently he lifted into the
air a huge board on which was chalked, "*Is that
the 'Pride of Wales'?*" Our affirmative pennant
was soon flying in the breeze. He then turned
the board round: "*Have urgent orders for you.*"
Our curiosity was intense. The Captain was hot
on the scent when he surmised it was probably
a change of destination, for all along he thought
Portsmouth sounded wrong for a merchant ship
to discharge phosphate rock at. We envisaged
beating up the Channel for some of the North-
European ports, which meant another week at sea.

A stoutly-built Cornish fishing boat, with the
Penzance registration letters prominently displayed
on her beam, was closing swiftly under our lee.
There was a brisk sea running, for it was blowing
fresh, and the Atlantic swell was in evidence.
It did not seem to bother these five placid and
unmoved fisher folk. Nosing their craft cleverly
into our main chains and waiting a second or two
until the two ships were on the same level, a fisherman stepped aboard with the grace of a fairy.
The fishing boat then stood off. It compared favour-
ably with us for seaworthiness. It was built of
mighty timbers. The man told us of the great
excitement on board the lugger when they sighted
a barque far away on the horizon and wondered
if she were their quest, then of losing her in a
heavy snow squall and the consequent disappointment. Benefiting by the smart breeze, they made

to cut off the barque's chance of escape, and then finding the very ship they wanted in a clear patch just a mile away.

The skipper proceeded to unfold a poster, which he said had been displayed in shop windows at the Cornish ports. We read the following:

£10 REWARD

Whereas the Barque *Pride of Wales* due in the English Channel between the 25th of April and the 5th of May has been wrongly ordered to proceed to Portsmouth, the above reward will be paid to any person or persons able to intercept the said ship before she reaches the longitude of the Eddystone lighthouse and instruct her to make for Plymouth, her correct port of destination.

It will be noticed that the owner was most exacting in his dates, for this was the 5th of May. The Cornish skipper was a welcome guest, and the Captain made much fuss of him. He loved our rum and polished off two half-tumblerfuls in two gulps. His pockets were soon bulging with plug tobacco too. He had brought many blessings. The most important was a check on our position, for the leaden skies of the last three days had precluded accurate observations by means of sun or stars. He, the fisherman, had seen the light of Bishop's Rock early that morning, which put our computations almost dead accurate.

The news that the end of our passage was a hundred and fifty miles nearer was much relished. "Plymouth Sound to-morrow" was a pleasant reflection. Taking his depature with the same ease and delicacy of step, he must have returned to his craft pleased with life. He had found the *Pride of*

Wales on the high seas. This was an achievement of major importance when it is considered that anything from fifty to a hundred other fishing boats were on the lookout for us as well. He had a chit in his pocket worth £10. His pluck in coming out a hundred miles from the Lizard was rewarded. Hurling half a hundred fresh mackerel on our decks, which was, to our way of thinking, the greatest blessing of all, they continued with their toil, puffing away happily at their pipes and waving their greetings. We had to fly a special flag on the fore to notify other fishing vessels that we had been intercepted.

II

PLYMOUTH SOUND

Filling on the main-yards and setting every rag we possessed, we were off in a happy mood to polish off the last lap of the journey. We all helped the cook to prepare the toothsome mackerel for dinner. We were much too hungry to wait while they were being fried. Besides, it would mean giving up our rations of butter, which had run very low, before this could be done. Three dozen wonderful fish were pitched into a dixie and boiled in salt water. For delicacy of flavour I can thoroughly recommend this method of cooking mackerel. It would suit the most critical of tastes.

At ten that night we picked up the loom of the Lizard light far away to the nor'ard. We spent the remainder of the night beating hard to get close to the land. Sighting the bluff headlands guarding Plymouth Sound, they presented a strange appearance—under a mantle of snow on the 6th of May.

Port Castries, Island of St. Lucia

Pride of Wales called here for stores

Homeward bound through mighty seas

We came to terms with a tug-boat off the breakwater, which delivered us safely at Cattwater in
great style.

We clubbed together enough money to rig Jeff
up for his journey to London. We doubted very
much whether he would find any one to welcome
him, as his information about his people's doings
and whereabouts were vague in the extreme.
Asked by the Captain if he was glad to be back
in England, he replied that he would be pleased
with any land after that experience of the sea.
He was very particular about the clothes we
bought him. He wanted to look like a sailor, and
thought he was entitled to. His appearance excited
much mirth in the fo'c'sle. I saw him off at the
station. Dressed in a black fisherman's cap with
sides that could be lowered over the ears in bad
weather, a white muffler tied in a big knot, a heavy
double-reefer jacket, blue trousers with plenty of
room in them, and a stout pair of new boots, and
10s. in his pocket, he looked a strange vision.
Tears filled my eyes as the train steamed off with
this tragic human once again adrift in the world.

o

CHAPTER IX

A Cruise De Luxe

I

A CHRONOMETER ERROR

MY third voyage in the *Pride of Wales* was a cruise de luxe. If there had been a competition among sailors of the old sailing-ship days for the most delightful voyage, I feel sure that the one I am about to describe would be well in the running. The great feature of the trip was that it was short, yet full of variety and experience. We sailed from England on the last day of June, 1891, and we were home again on the last day of December of the same year. In that time we visited three islands only, one in the South Atlantic and two in the West Indies, covering a total distance of about thirteen thousand miles. Except for about ten days at the end we had glorious weather and continuous sunshine.

Bound for the lonely island of Ascension with Government stores, we took our departure from the Longship lighthouse off Land's End. The only man who seemed unhappy on this beautiful day was the Captain; and confiding in me with rather more freedom that usual, he divulged the reason for his disturbed state of mind. It appeared that his true and trusty friend, the ship's chronometer, which had been taken ashore during our stay in

England to undergo the periodic overhaul, had been returned by the expert with a certificate purporting to show that the old error which the chronometer had enjoyed for years no longer existed, but that a new one had been established which was curiously enough the same rate but directly opposite. There was really every excuse for alarm. Had the expert made an error? On any other voyage such doubts could have been dealt with lightly by looking forward to a reasonable margin in the land-fall, but on this occasion accuracy was all essential, for the small island of Ascension stands in the South Atlantic, seven hundred miles from the nearest land, and was notorious for its elusiveness to a sailing ship coming from England, first of all by reason that it could only be approached from the one direction—from south-east; and again the island could not be found at night because it was not lighted in any way; and lastly it might be, and quite frequently was, hidden from any distant view by mist.

Much more disconcerting was a feature always uppermost in the navigator's mind that if he did miss his mark it meant making a detour of 2,500 miles before he could have another opportunity of trying to find it, for in view of the powerful equatorial current running in the same direction as the wind, the task of beating back, once it had been passed, was hopelessly impossible. There were instances recorded showing that the island had been missed by sailing ships, and we were warned of the danger. This was the voyage when the ship *British Isles* beat us so badly in the Portuguese trades. It was strange that we did not on that occasion ask the *British Isles* for a check of position, but I suppose the skipper felt sufficiently humiliated without having his navigation powers challenged as well.

Anxiety increased when we came to the Equator to find ourselves alone at a place where generally many vessels were to be seen, and we had been eagerly looking forward to the occasion, so as to check position with passing ships; but no luck came our way until we had been forty days out, and this time it was nearly bad luck. Had it been night, we might easily have been piled up on some unknown coral reef off the Brazilian shores.

Seamen working on the fore-yard reported a change in the colour of the sea, and that they had seen branches and leaves of tropical trees floating by and other signs of the proximity of land. The truth was now out; the new chronometer rating was wrong. What was one to do? Land was not in sight, nor could we get soundings with our meagre methods at two hundred fathoms.

The Captain, now on the horns of a dilemma, took the only course that suggested itself, and from that instant he went back to the chronometer's old timing and made for the spot in the ocean where we should have been under the old conditions, and hoped for the best. This was all most disconcerting, for really to all intents and purposes we had no idea where we were, and with three thousand miles more before us, of which some 18° were longitude.

2

A MAJESTIC LANDFALL

Having cleared the south-east trade and run down a sort of easting through the south-west monsoons until we arrived again in the south-east trade on the St. Helena-Ascension route, we eventually arrived at a spot calculated to be a hundred and fifty miles south-east of Ascension, the last and fateful twenty-four anxious hours of the passage which had lasted sixty odd days. Excitement ran high, and betting with plugs of tobacco was rife throughout the ship. Would we make a land-fall or not? Heaving-to about midnight in order to leave the last forty or fifty miles for daylight the next day, scarcely a man closed his eyes, and we roamed about the decks peering in every direction into the darkness.

Just at break of day our hearts were set throbbing at the appearance of a hideous-looking bird on the upper top sail-yard arm—hideous because of its untidy plumage and excited expressions. At any other time this intruder would have been looked upon as an omen of bad luck, and that an ill-starred sailor would make a footslip from that yard and fall to his doom. But an old salt among the crew knew it to be a frigate bird, and said that it never roamed far from land.

This good news gladdened our gloomy hearts immensely. Having rested a while and tidied his ruffled feathers, our wary friend took off and flew in exactly the direction that we were steering. How wonderful are the homing instincts of the feathered world! Extra lookouts were posted on the fo'c'sle head and the fore-yards. Necks craned and eyes peered into the morning mist, and as the crimson sun rose into the heaven so the mist of night faded, leaving a silver shimmer between the deep blue of sea and sky. Another perfect day had come to greet us.

Far away on the distant horizon rested a solitary cloud. Was it a land cloud? Was it hiding from us our goal? The light and shade of its substance was being continuously re-shaped before our straining eyes, as if manipulated by the magic of a divine hand, compressing, lifting, and tearing apart until the last unsubstantial fragments vanished to reveal the silhouette of a little world that had so anxiously been our quest. "Land ahead, sir," sang out the lookout man on the top-gallant yard. What a proud moment for the Captain. Such a majestic land-fall seemed a fitting and crowning reward for a courageous mariner.

3

ASCENSION

The strenuous work of hauling up from the cable-lockers the usual hundred fathoms for each anchor, and catting both anchors in readiness for dropping, kept me busy in the chain-locker knocking the kinks out of the cable to give it a fair lead through the deck pipe; but when I did come on deck the island was only about five miles away, and I must say I thought it was a weird-looking place. It reminded me of the original of some fantastic greeting card, sort of "hands-across-the-sea" affair. The rugged eminences and irregular slopes, cul-

minating into a solitary peak which crept many
hundreds of feet into the heavens, seemed bare
and bereft of any kind of vegetation; and when
one considered that the island was situated in a
climate unequalled for charm and delight where the
heat of the tropical sun was tempered by a continuous and delicious breeze, it seemed all wrong,
to say the least, not to see a tree or a meadow.
But when the heavy morning mist had lifted to
uncover the higher part of the mountain, it was
found that the summit was covered with a rich
green that looked so unnatural against the drab
surroundings that it might have been artificially
painted. I will later describe a visit paid to this
peak where words are wholly inadequate to express
the wonderful animal and vegetable life that exists
on this cloud-swept height. On the extreme right
was a small dome-shaped island a few cable lengths
from the main island, marble white in colour and
a perfectly smooth-looking surface, which put a
finishing touch to an awesome panorama.

If one could imagine standing on the bed of the
ocean in this region, Ascension would appear from
the oozy wildness (covering thousands of square
miles) a towering volcanic mountain rising perpendicularly and ruggedly fifteen thousand feet,
about four times the height of Snowdon. It forms
a part of no visible continent, the nearest land being
the other lonely island of St. Helena, seven hundred
miles distant. Ascension is a sentinel guarding the
dignity of its own impressive solitude.

It was necessary, in order to make sure of getting
to our destination, to hug the island as close as
possible, for had we made a wide sweep, by the time
the lee side was reached where the Garrison of

Georgetown was situated, we might find the wind. erratic and disappear altogether, due to the high weather shore. Should our position be too far out at sea and then meet these conditions, it would be good-bye to Ascension for at least two weeks, if not more. The current would sweep us away.

4

THE BOATSWAIN BIRD

When we were quite close to the white island, we were amazed to find that the colour and smooth surface it enjoyed was due to its being packed with a white bird known as the "boatswain bird," a very pretty and graceful sea bird about the size of an ordinary gull, with a brick-coloured beak and yellow legs and two long pointed feathers forming the tail. It received its name from sailors, for when on the wing it uttered a shrill cry which reminded the sailor of the boatswain's whistle. The birds seemed quite unperturbed by our proximity to their sanctuary, but most unfortunately for us it became necessary to strike four bells, and this was what some of them probably had never heard before. It brought disquietude among the junior members, for instantaneously the whole island seemed to rise on wings, so many birds were there that the land was hidden from view. Would they pay us a visit? They did, and it was a scene never to be forgotten. We were entirely cut off from land, sea, and sun. Amid the indescribable chorus and their piercing shrieks it was useless to give an order. We just looked at each other like idiots.

The air was charged with a fishy smell which was wafted across our faces by their million wings. I have heard it said that it is considered lucky to have one's wearing apparel soiled by a bird flying overhead. There was ample evidence on this ocasion that Dame Fortune wished us to enjoy a long spell of her magic blessing.

Here, too, appeared in goodly numbers our old friend of the early morning, the frigate bird, also I presume named by sailors because of the aggressive and audacious manner he displayed when in search of food. He is an out-and-out thief, and one would on first thoughts associate his methods with some creature possessed of a lazy and indolent disposition, but not so the frigate bird. His insatiable appetite kept him occupied almost continuously, and working at high pressure. He would watch other birds diligently collecting their food, then quite suddenly he would sally forth to the fray, chase them with great rapidity and determination, and harass them to such an extent that they would be forced to let go in mid-air a choice fish. Then the robber, checking his speed and direction cleverly, would swoop down most gracefully after the spoil and secure it without any doubt while it was still falling. Curiously enough, when he did rest, he would settle down in a perfectly friendly manner with the birds that he had actually robbed.

Having rounded the last headland, we opened up the Garrison. The international code-signal "B.D."="What ship is that?" greeted us from the signalling station. "J.Q.P.N." was hoisted in reply, meaning *Pride of Wales*. Then, "Anchor on a bearing from this station and report" was next hoisted. This signal was obeyed sixty-four days after leaving England. Although sixty-four days was not long as voyages went in those days, it was surprising the amount of marine growth that had gathered and developed on the underwater sides of the ship in that short time. Barnacles three and four inches long could be counted in their hundreds of thousands, and as the ship lightens during the process of discharging, it is possible to clean the exposed hull to a little below sea level, but the lowermost parts remain until opportunities occur to beach or dry dock. However, within an hour of anchoring every barnacle had disappeared. The sea all round the ship was a bustling mass of fish of every size, kind, and colour. They loved our barnacles, and we were delighted to oblige them. By swinging a derrick over the side and lowering a ballast basket into the sea, we hoisted fish on board by the hundredweight in no time. What a sight, and what a relish for our salt-sodden digestions!

Ascension changed from French to British rule just at the end of the Napoleonic Wars, when Napoleon was brought a prisoner to St. Helena. It is 7° south of the Equator and a thousand miles from Sierra Leone, the nearest mainland. It was created a Naval Station and manned by officers and men of the Royal Navy and Royal Marines under the command of a Naval Captain. The personnel was about a hundred and fifty all ranks; and about the same number of West African natives were drafted in as servants and labourers.

5

SHORE LEAVE

Taking the Skipper ashore in the jolly-boat to report was an amusing business. There is no pretence at a harbour. It is just a very small Garrison town on a rocky shelf overlooking the bay. The pier where we had to land was a rocky bluff blasted to some sort of shape and filled with concrete to give it a flat effect. Steps were cut out of the face of the rock down to the sea, but they were useless, as the sea conditions rarely permitted boats to go near the land. It was necessary to moor the boat to a buoy and pay out enough rope to allow the boat to ride safely about ten yards from the bluff, then a crane was swung out and a template was lowered to within a few feet of the boat. Into this one leapt. It had no solid floor, so that if it were caught by a wave it would not capsize and throw the passenger out but would just fill with water from underneath and up to the passenger's waist. Gradually the template would be heaved up by a steam-power winch and swung landwards. All the stores brought to the island had to be landed in this manner, and it took five weeks to dispose of our small cargo.

Being the owner's grandson, I was allowed to land on this occasion. I frequently was conceded minor favours like this, whereas the others had to return with the boat. I felt very *gauche* and ill at ease as I strolled aimlessly on this inhospitable headland. First of all, my legs, after two months' incarceration on this tee-totum, barely functioned, and with each step the ground seemed to heave at me. With the exception of a very smart-looking marine doing police duty—who glanced slyly in my direction occasionally as if I were a suspect—there seemed little life just here; so I strolled slowly further inland, but always keeping my weather eye open for the Skipper.

Finding a place labelled "Naval Stores," I got into conversation with a dapper little man with a neatly-trimmed beard, wearing white naval kit. (Strangely enough, I met him again many years later when I paid a visit to Nelson's *Victory* at Portsmouth). He most kindly invited me to his bungalow to take tea, and described me to his wife and two young daughters, who were the only two girls on the island, as "a young fellow from the freighter in the Bay which has just come from England." I must have struck them as something very grim, for I was certainly not dressed for a tea-party: blue dungarees, sennit slippers, and an open shirt, with very begrimed hands and face.

In exchange for news from England I had a marvellous tea. My hunger precluded any attempt at table manners. I had three helpings of plum cake, and they assured me there would be plenty more the next day if I cared to go along. This wasn't too bad, to have met the only two girls on the island and partaken of a delicious homely tea within an hour of landing, besides receiving a pressing invitation to attend divine service with them on the following Sunday at the Naval Church. After tea they all walked with me down to the jetty, where I had the pleasure of introducing the Captain to them and, incidentally, the opportunity of paving the way to ask for leave on Sunday.

What struck me particularly, and also the

Captain, was the amazing number of rats that we
had seen running about. It appears that the whole
island was infested with them, and apparently
always had been, even to a point of being a
dangerous menace. In the early days of British
rule, flocks of cats were landed at various points
with the idea of exterminating the plague in this
way, but the cats refused to play. They much
preferred the wonderful fish and bird life of the '
island to the unwholesome rodent. But in a few
years a new pest had sprung up in the form of wild
cats, which grew to a much greater size than the
domestic variety. They are still on the island, and
afford good sport to the gun.

When the Captain acceded to my wish for shore
leave to attend divine service, I was finally convinced that his attitude towards me had become
much more friendly than had been the case during
the previous voyages, when I think he imagined
that a good deal of tittle-tattle about him and his
methods of command might have filtered to the
owner in my letters home, but after thirty-thou-
sand miles together he was inclined to the belief
that all was well. Unfortunately for me improvement in this direction reacted against me in another,
for it gave birth to bitter feelings of jealousy on the
part of the Chief Mate, whose conception of
discipline was of the martinettish variety. I could
see that the necessity of manning the boat purposely
to take a boy ashore on Sunday would severely
strain the already delicate situation, but the Captain,
with extreme dexterity, at breakfast on Sunday
morning said to the Chief: "Hughes is the only
person in the ship who has asked for shore leave
to attend divine service. I have been guilty of

making many disagreeable decisions against sailors
in my life, but I have never yet been known to
prevent one from attending divine service. So,
Mr. Jones, get the boat ready to take Hughes
ashore."

The four stalwarts detailed to man the boat
were alive to the amusing incident. The small
church, like all the other buildings in the Garrison,
was Service-built, and they were very proud of
the spire. It was unique, to say the least, as it was
built entirely of disused biscuit tins.

6

TURTLES

I was greatly interested in the visit we paid
after dinner to the turtle ponds. The island was
famous for turtle. When their season was due they
would come in large numbers from the heart of the
ocean, often hundreds of miles away, to seek the
seclusion of the island's sandy beaches where they
laid their eggs. One marvels at the uncanny
instincts they possess, which enable them to
navigate their way with such unfailing accuracy
over the tractless sea. Their visit to the beaches
is fraught with much anxiety. Watchers, who
have taken up positions in concealed places, spring
upon them and turn them on their backs with
amazing dexterity. This operation disarms them
completely of any offensive or defensive intentions.
They are then carted to the ponds ready for ship-
ment home, where they provide the table of the
gastronome with a delicacy all too rare. Their
motherhood is a curious affair, and probably quite

unique. The mother turtle makes a hole in the
sand, with her handy flippers, large enough to
accommodate herself and the hundred eggs she
intends to lay. The egg is about the size of a billiard
ball, quite round and white in colour, but the
shell is soft. The process of laying takes about
two days. The eggs are then carefully covered
over with sand. Then the turtle makes again for
the open sea, and so ends her maternal responsi-
bilities. Her lot is not to know the fate of her
offspring nor to nurture them in their tender days.
The young turtle is one of the sweetest things
imaginable to look at and to hold in one's hand.
It is perfectly formed and finished at the moment
it leaves the egg. One is filled with admiration at
the plucky way in which he sets out alone on life's
great venture.

After the life-giving rays of the sun have brought
the eggs to fruition, the little fellows battle their
way to the surface of the sand. They quickly take
stock of the strange surroundings, then hurriedly
make for the sea. From the moment they first
see daylight their little lives are beset with peril
and anxiety, and although many scores leave the
nest few of them survive to reach the sea. Vulturous villains of the air, always relishing this
delicacy, wait patiently during the period of in-
cubation and swoop down on the little mites as
they waddle to their element. Those that gain
the open sea anxiously make for the first patch of
seaweed, where they wisely remain for many
months and hide, for they dare not leave until
their protective covering has toughened sufficiently
to withstand the hard life that is ahead of them.
If they get through this period safely, then they

are destined to live more years than are allotted to man and to grow to an enormous size, often weighing from three to four hundred pounds.

7

WIDE-AWAKE FAIR

The island, measuring only seven miles by five, made it possible to see most of the sights and return the same day. Wide-Awake Fair we were told we must see.

The scene of the excitement was a sandy plain four miles away. And to imagine a space about the size of Rushmoor Arena of Tattoo fame filled with eggs only a few inches apart, with an attending mother in close watch over each, will give an idea of the amazing sight. The "wide-awake" or "sooty tern" is a sea bird about the size of a small gull, with white breast and black or soot-coloured back. It visits the island regularly to lay one egg and hatch it. The name "wide-awake" is given because the cry of the bird resembles the pronunciation of the words almost exactly.

The only way to get to the "Fair" was on foot, and a walk of eight miles would not appear insurmountable; but there could never be a more punishing journey. Rarely did we find anything resembling a path after the first mile or so, and for three hours we were jumping from crag to clinker, from clinker to crater, scaling precipitous ravines lined with lava, and trundling across barren wastes of dusty ash which was blown into our moist faces by gusts of hot wind. We saw one solitary tree, a palm—evidently planted for a wager.

We had been told by the Marines before starting (rather reversing the order of things) that they had pegged out a space from which all the eggs had been cleared, so that any that were in this enclosed area on our arrival would be new-laid and fit to bring away.

The sight of this gigantic assembly of birds was bewildering. Astonishing, too, was the tameness of the birds. One would expect wild birds, quite unaccustomed to humanity, to be rather timid; but not so the "wide-awake." I believe they must have thought that we were part of their natural surroundings.

Morris, the dare-devil of the party, penetrated deeply into the colony, and it was a curious sight to watch his movements picking his way cautiously between the eggs. His form was soon surrounded and completely hidden from view by disturbed birds, and only those birds in the immediate track that he was taking took to wing as he advanced. The birds in his wake settled down again as if nothing had happened. All we could see was a column of cackling "wide-awakes" about ten feet high, moving slowly amongst the myriads of others. The Captain said it reminded him of the movement of a water-spout in miniature. Apparently it was the first time that day that Morris had felt cool, for not only was he sheltered from the sun, but he was continuously fanned by the birds' wings, which actually brushed his face. Some settled on his shoulders and pecked gently at his ears, others preferred his cap.

They say that it was a wonderful sight when the colony of "wide-awakes" was arranging to leave the island. There was much commotion and

P

excitement, and when they moved off, that part of the island was darkened by their numbers. One can imagine the chatter! Their departure was a sad loss to the wild-animal life of the island, for they must have relished the continuous feast of new-laid eggs within such easy reach.

8

GREEN MOUNTAIN

When we first arrived at the island, so alluring did Green Mountain appear that almost every one expressed a desire to climb to the top, but when the day came the party had whittled down to two, Morris and myself, and I believe that we stuck to our guns because it would give us the excuse to have the whole day on shore.

First a word or two about Green Mountain. Necessity had prompted the Garrison to a determined effort to turn to useful purpose the only part of the island that offered the possibility of any measure of agricultural success. The development of the Peak started with the early days of British occupation, for they were short of many of the fresh necessities of life, such as water, meat, vegetables, fruit, and dairy produce. Of fish there was always plenty. The rest had to be created. These amateurs of the Royal Navy and Marines achieved remarkable success as farmers on the top of this mountain, where their cattle-rearing, general farming, construction of houses, institutions and farm buildings, walls and reservoirs, pipe-laying and quarrying, testified to their ability. Still more does it redound to their credit when it is considered that the whole personnel changed about every three years. They had to contend with geological conditions much the same as existed all over the island—ravines, rugged spurs, huge craters, boulders, clinker, sulphurous deposits, cinders and ash; but there was the only comforting difference, moisture was here in abundance, and that is why their efforts were concentrated at the mountain top. Almost daily scudding clouds slashed against the rugged eminence high up, to be transformed into torrential and welcome rain, which they conserved in huge concrete tanks. Even in the dry season, moisture in the form of dew was trapped and collected and turned to useful service.

Our climb over the arid lower slopes was dusty, tiring, and tedious, but having reached the thousand-feet mark we enjoyed the cooler air. The pleasing sight of vegetation brought comfort and courage to our hearts. It was plain to see that our efforts were to be richly rewarded, for the day was beautifully clear. Looking down on that desolate volcanic mass, it suddenly seemed to have changed and to have assumed a rugged grandeur which blended harmoniously with the verdant crown of the tall mountain. Man's mastery over physical difficulties was now becoming evident. We had passed from waste and desolation into a graceful oasis. Every scrap of tableland was utilised. Earth brought from England and tropical countries was scattered, seed was sown wherever possible, with the result that we saw English cattle grazing and thriving amidst rustic surroundings of unequalled charm. They have here no winter rigours to withstand, for every dawn brings a summer day, every dusk the refreshing dew. Close at hand, well-groomed horses in first-class condition were tugging a load of root crop up a steep hill. Here were farm buildings that would vie with Surrey's best. Poultry wandered about and cackled in the happiest of moods. Sheep grazed on what appeared to be impossible gradients, with a Shepherd Marine in close attendance lest ill might befall them.

We looked down on a charming cottage set in a blaze of bloom and blossom all artificially produced, with a view of unrivalled splendour overlooking the whole island, and the infinite ocean extending in a rich blue to the distant horizon. Large shade-giving cabbage trees, mingling artistically with tropical pine and palm, formed a portion of the garden. Moss, ferns, and rock roses grew in terraced profusion. Richly-tinted English and tropical birds twittered from bough to branch in a merriment of song. Close at hand pheasants, too, proudly strutted over stubbled field. Soil had been imported also from Brazil to suit the development of orange, guava, lime, banana and other tropical fruit trees; and from all appearance they seemed to thrive.

In climbing close on two thousand feet we had rounded thirty ramps and corners, and although at times dusty and fatiguing, it was always wonderfully interesting, with wild tomatoes and Australian wattle everywhere. Leaning on a ramp wall high up in the skies and looking in a westerly direction, the view was magnificent. There were innumerable craggy cones, each a crater, divided one from the other by deep and rugged gorges. On the extreme left was an extra big one known as the Devil's Riding School, and it was well named.

Wild goats roamed in numbers amongst these terrifying heights.

Far away, riding serenely on the still sea, we could espy the little craft that had brought us there; she was the only ship in the place. In a large harbour like Rio de Janeiro we felt rather ashamed of her insignificance among the bevy of three-thousand-ton full-riggers, but this day, in her loneliness, the *Pride of Wales* fitted in well with the scheme of desolation, and we were proud of her. When we reached the dusty roads of the lower levels, foot-sore and tired, it was difficult to reconcile the inhospitable clinker cinders and ash which seemed to fill all available spaces with the paradise of Green Mountain. We felt we had been to another world, and one possessing great charm and beauty, but we failed to convince the boat's crew who fetched us that we had been to heaven, for we were begrimed from head to foot with a dirty rust-coloured dust which, owing to the heat of the day, had caked on the exposed part of our bodies, leaving only the whites of our eyes and our feverish-coloured lips to break the monotony. They thought by our appearance that we had come from the other place.

9

FISH

We used to enjoy going to the rich fishing grounds about a quarter of a mile away from our anchorage, where we rarely had an abortive visit, for so plentiful was the fish and so generously did it surrender that the subtle art lost much of its charm and cunning. We used to set off in two boats just after dark, armed with iron belaying pins, an axe, hurricane lamps, and, of course, fishing tackle. The two former implements were needed to deal with the wild capers of the conger, which invariably formed a good proportion of the catch, and so huge were they that they even compelled amateur anglers to be truthful. It was no uncommon occurrence to secure one measuring ten feet. One could always tell when a big conger was on. This meant bringing the two boats together so as to get plenty of man power to deal with the devils. What a terrifying sight, and what a bloody battle as seen in the dim light of a hurricane lamp, with the conger and his staring ugly eyes, his long cavernous and foaming mouth filled with ferocious-looking teeth, squirming and leaping with rage. But once we had got him jammed between the two boats his number was up. The axe and belaying pins were soon in action.

Garfish, too, was an easy victim. . In fact this little fish needed neither hook nor line. As a rule they used to gambol on the surface in great numbers, threading through each other daintily, very much interested in our presence in their midst. Their uncommon appearance and their rich greenish-blue colour were fascinating to a degree. Garfish possess a delicate flavour, and their bones, when cooked, turn green, which is most helpful when one is in a hurry. Another amusing fish was the "soldier," an all-red variety with a fierce expression. He was quite nice, however, on the table.

One day we had great fun, which brought the ship's work to a standstill. We watched with wild excitement a school of bonito raiding the bay.

Fish of every description, size, and colour were driven into a feverish frenzy. The sea resembled a shimmering lake of silver tinted here and there with streaks of gold and shades of green. Some contortioned in wild leaps, others sped along the surface of the sea at great speed in an endeavour to escape. The attack was on a wide front, with our ship much in the centre, so not only did we get an excellent view, but we also reaped a harvest, for many fish crashed against the ship's side in their blind rush to escape and remained stunned and helpless on the surface. The attackers worked their way systematically shorewards, and within a short time the beach was littered with many tons of dead fish. Rather a peaceful end than torture.

It was never safe to go too far from the ship after dark, for the island was visited by mighty ocean rollers. They came without warning, but during the day they could be seen approaching. They were horrible things, and crashed against the rocky shores for days at a time, making communication between ship and shore quite impossible. They resembled a continuity of huge billows, and completely overwhelmed the ordinary waves. Their terror was intensified because they came in two varieties, single and double. Their arrival brought the island's maritime life to a standstill. They also drove everyone away from the foreshores and beaches. They were supposed to be progressive undulations of waves resulting from storms in the distant oceans.

One curious thing about Ascension was that it had but few beaches of any note or size. Far away on the weather side was, however, one

possessed of great charm and beauty known as Crystal
Bay, where the whole strand was formed of crystal
of many hues, bright and vivid; green, ruby,
yellow, and violet particles glistened in the sun. It
was like a garden of precious stones. Another, which
contained the remnants of a wreck, was known
as Dead Man's Beach. Then came Comfortless
Cove, named after a tragic occasion when the little
beach was used as a burial ground for unfortunate
victims of yellow fever. Ascension, by virtue of
its healthy situation, was years ago used as a
sanatorium, where Service people from the then
unhealthy Stations of West Africa, a thousand
miles away, were sent to recuperate. A transport
was once despatched on one of these merciful
errands, but tragedy befell it on the long voyage
across. Yellow fever broke out, and on her arrival
at Ascension, in order to safeguard the Garrison,
she was placed in quarantine off this small cove.
Here matters became much worse and many died.
They were buried reverently on the beach of what
was afterwards named Comfortless Cove. Lastly,
Long Beach, which was the largest, and faced our
anchorage. It was here that all the fish were piled
up on the beach after the bonito raid.

Recently I had the pleasure of meeting a Mr.
Gadd, a retired Royal Marine Light Infantryman,
who served extremely happy years on the island.
When I told him that I was mentioning Ascension
in my sea reminiscences, he hoped I would not
leave out South-West Bay, but as I had not been
there he very kindly told me all about it. South
West Bay was a delightful cove not far from the
solitary coconut tree on the way to Wide Awake.
Here there had been found to exist in plenty a

species of limestone, and as lime is an essential
commodity wherever Naval barracks and buildings
are to be found, the little place lost a good deal
of its charm and became an active quarrying centre.
Two Marines were detailed to operate there continuously. They lived in a stone hut and were not
required to return to the Garrison. Their rations,
including water, were sent there daily on a pack
donkey, in charge of a Kruboy. They settled
down to the work in a contented manner and
became perfectly happy, and thoroughly enjoyed
the freedom that the banishment had created. It
was quite fashionable to walk from the Garrison
on Sunday afternoons to take tea and talk with
these merry Marines. When Gadd was there the
two monarchs were busily engaged in decorating
the interior of their castle. They had a unique
scheme of wall decoration—paper or limewash
was much too commonplace. They had collected
an endless variety of dainty sea shells which they
blended in artistic colour schemes and applied to
the walls in their inimitable style. Their peaceful
and aboriginal existence was disturbed by the shrill
whistle of an Admiralty tug, towing a lighter
manned by many Krumen. They had called for
a cargo of limestone.

Although a British Garrison bears an unmistakable stamp no matter in what part of the world
it may be, the inclusion of a hundred and fifty
negroes from the West Coast of Africa gave
Ascension a touch of its rightful atmosphere. Of
this number most of them were Krumen. "Kru,"
I think, means "free." They were drafted from
the coast of Liberia. These men are noted for
their skill as surf sailors, and were probably

selected for this reason. They were quartered in a part of the garrison which was given the name Krutown. Here they were allowed to enjoy a similar life to what they were accustomed to in their native Liberia. They were very happy, and loved the life on the island. To them it was "a little bit of heaven."

H.M.S. *Wye*, a vessel specially appointed to the service of Ascension, was a store and troop ship combined, and visited the island twice a year. One of her duties was to call at Sierra Leone to transport these native drafts. They were recruited and enlisted in the usual naval manner and served like every one else for three years. During the process of enrolment it was found that their bush names were long and impossible. So they were invited to choose an English name. They invariably chose those of famous men such as William Shakespeare, Oliver Cromwell, Charles Dickens, John Bunyan, David Livingstone, and so on. Frequently these names became exhausted. Then the M.O. getting inspiration by glancing round the ship, would suggest. His suggestions were gladly accepted, so that the roll contained such names as the following: Bill Derrick, Jack Funnel, Jimmy Mast, Bob Dodger, Teddy Bell, etc.

I was privileged to visit Krutown, and much enjoyed the occasion. My escort was a civilian— the only one on the island. He was appointed as a civilian representative of the Government. He brought several Kruboys to close quarters, so that I could see the tribal markings, mostly on their foreheads. These markings distinguish tribes, and indicated in this instance that they had been liberated from slavedom. The food habits of the

Kru were strange in the extreme—meat and fish rations as soon as issued were hoisted up a long pole away from the reach of wild cats and rats. These poles were outside their quarters and were far from decorative. The food remained there, exposed to the rays of the tropical sun, until it reached an advanced stage of putrefaction. The visit of flies and mosquitoes in their hordes to the top of the pole was not discouraged. They probably gave additional piquancy to the joint.

We noticed a happy group squatting; one of them was working hard trying to get music out of an old accordion. The bellows were covered with adhesive plaster and stamp paper, and even then it did not hold the air long enough to produce the all-essential bass notes. I told my escort, Mr. Allen, that I would like to make them a present of mine, which was practically new. Did he think it would be appreciated? "Well," he replied, "if you do, you will be the subject matter of their most ardent prayers until it wears out."

That night our attention was attracted to much commotion alongside. Looking over the rail, we saw in the moonlight, peeping up from the sea, the cheerful faces of many negroes. They had called for the accordion. It filled my heart with delight to see the appreciative expression on each face in turn as they ran their black fingers along the keys of this wonderful maker of mirth. The negroes became fond of English games and acquitted themselves well when "Ascension Day," the festive day of the year, came round. This was given up almost entirely to sport and entertainments.

The Garrison was proud of the quality of its cricket, and men boasted they had not lost a match for years. The boast was safe, for they could only play representative cricket when a Battleship or a Cruiser called in, and that only happened at very infrequent intervals. It was their only hope for a match. The nearest land team was at St. Helena, seven hundred miles away.

I was invited to play in a match—this was a compliment paid to English people who happened to call there in strange ships. I think I was unpopular with the spectators, for I caught out "the draw"—a young marine who was a prodigious slogger and gave much entertainment when at the wicket.

Running across the longfield—my eyes glued on the small ball high up in the sky—I got mixed up with spectators (sailors and marines). As I approached them, I could hear remarks directed at me in scorching language: "Who the 'ell is this bloke? Bet you a bob he doesn't get near it," etc. But I could see it as big as a feather pillow, and they were filled with wrath. The pitch was concrete, and the stumps were stuck in a small bed of clay. The outfield was volcanic ash. I went in to bat at close of day, and only had to face one ball. Fortunately for me, it was off the wicket; had it been straight it must have killed me. A lithe lank fair-haired youth of the Navy could send them down like a shell out of a three-pounder. He ran much like an ostrich. I was spared further distress by the arrival of darkness which fell on the island every day all through the year, almost exactly at six. It came with amazing suddenness.

That night I was invited to a boxing tournament. As is usual when the Services foregather, the quality of the sport reached a high standard. My partner at the wicket earlier was now in the ring. His skill here was much more pronounced. He knocked the captain of our side in the afternoon through the ropes, remarking that he deserved it for putting him so low down the batting list.

Our sojourn at the island ended all too soon. It was one of those places that possessed the realism of a fantastic dream. Such a visit made one feel proud of one's nationality. It provided undeniable evidence of our ability as a race to settle down in a happy mood and contented manner in many parts of the world and under most conditions.

.   .   .   .   .

We had received orders before leaving England to proceed from Ascension to Barbados in the West Indies, where we would receive further sailing instructions. This meant a run of over two thousand miles across the tropical Atlantic, hugging the Equator, first the south side and then the north side.

CHAPTER X

SEA SHANTY

I

SPERM WHALE

WHEN we sailed from Ascension we were escorted by a sperm whale. He kept an exemplary station on our port beam and seemed quite friendly. Far away to the southward we could see many more almost in a cluster. They seemed to be having a happy time, for they were spouting and dashing about playfully and going our way. One of our A.B.s had spent a long time in a whaling ship, and he was full of interesting information about their lives and habits. His version was that our big friend was, in reality, watching us in case we would interfere with his harem of young cow whales in the offing. Had we incurred his displeasure we should have known something about it. A creature his size was capable of destroying, by a series of vicious attacks, quite a large-sized vessel. He seemed disinclined to abandon his watchful eye on us until a late hour in the night. His head was terrific, and measured about a third of the entire body, with a blunt and powerful nose, one which could command a deal of respect should eventualities arise to annoy him. We computed his length to be in the region of seventy feet.

2

INTERLUDE AT THE WHEEL

Our meagre amount of ballast—forty tons only, instead of at least eighty—compelled us to place in the hold, to help the stiffening, every conceivable thing that could be spared during the passage. The reason for taking so little ballast was governed by its price, 10s. per ton. These parsimonious measures were necessary if profit was to be made; so for two days we were busy hauling the heavy anchors and the two hundred and twenty fathoms of cable, weighing many tons, and laying them on the ballast. Mooring chains, kedge anchors, two boats, spare spars, derricks, and heavy stores also found their way below on the sand. For a fortnight the entire crew were hard at it, chipping the rust off the iron parts of the hold, including the thousand-gallon water tank, and cleaning the shackle pins of the cable. The men rather liked this, for with the hatches off it was quite a pleasant spot to be in during such hot weather.

In order to expedite this important work, I was excused my night watch and was kept on deck from dawn to dark. Most of this time I was entrusted with the steering of the ship. This released three men on one watch and four on the other during the hours of daylight, and in consequence much work was got through. There is something very arresting about steering a square-rigged vessel when under full sail. There is a feeling which gives the utmost thrill and pleasure —it is much like driving a spirited horse. It is almost magical how swiftly and obediently a ship responds to the will of man.

We were now running across the tropical summer at its height. The sun, the wind, the sea, the current, and the ship were all going from an easterly direction to a westerly. It was exceedingly hot, and no cooling effect can materialise from the breeze when dead astern, but it was very lovely. We seemed to have the world to ourselves, for no passing ships broke the solitude of our lives. Even the air seemed strange without the wail of the gull. We were passing through a Valhalla, far away from any land. It knew not the rage of the storm nor the wrath of the tempest. Eternal blue sea and cloudless sky, sunshine and summer, ruled this realm. And so I dreamed as I steered. Suddenly I would be awakened from my reverie by the Captain's shrill voice: "Wake up there! What part of the world are you taking us to now, my boy?" The ship was badly off her course.

3

BOAT ADRIFT

I will now explain how disaster can befall sailors and ships even under such ideal conditions as these, when normally one would think nothing could conceivably go wrong, short of some one committing an outrageous act.

An A.B., cleaning his plate in the usual sailor fashion by scooping over the side his half-eaten salt junk, espied a large turtle with flippers outstretched, asleep on the surface of the sea quite close to the ship. Having envied the gourmet so

much when gazing at those stout creatures basking
in the sun in the ponds at Ascension, waiting to
be shipped to a window in the Strand, we required
little persuasion in making a bold attempt at
landing this one for ourselves.

The only boat available was an old one resting
on the after skids, which had not seen the water
for some time, but had been reverently enshrouded
in canvas to keep the sun's rays from parching
its timbers. Hurriedly marking the spot with a
buoy, the ship was brought sharply into the wind.
The old boat was torn from its grips and swung
into the davits, then the cream of our crew
jumped in and were lowered into the sea and
cast adrift. They rowed feverishly along the curved
wake of the ship, directed by the Captain, who
had scampered up the rigging and had his eye on
the buoy.

The *modus operandi* when the boat had reached
the scene had been hurriedly discussed before
leaving the ship. It was to place a sling chain on
boat-hooks and pass a bight quickly over the
reptile's for'ard flipper. It would then be possible
to haul his head close enough in to effect the kill.
The approach to the sleeping quarry was a ticklish
procedure, for no one knew the intensity of his
slumber. The dipping oars scarcely ruffled the
sea. As the range closed, so the atmosphere became
eerie and tense. Their hearts sank when they
actually saw his size, much larger than he looked
from the ship's deck. A terrific fight seemed
imminent, but the turtle could have dealt quite
comfortably with half a dozen more sailors.
Although the sling chain was successfully placed
in position, once the monster realised what the

game was he parried each move with resolute determination. He first of all stoved in a plank and smashed the rudder with the secured flipper. He then shot off at a tangent and pulled the half water-logged gig over on its beam ends. Oars and capstan bars whirled through the air and crashed against his rock-like back. The spray flew high, but the crew quickly decided that if they didn't let go they would soon be shark's food. The turtle disappeared and took with him as a memento of the "brush up" a wrought-iron curb bracelet. Meantime much perturbation searched the minds of those left on board the *Pride of Wales*. It had been realised that the ship, due to insufficient ballast, had drifted an alarming distance from the boat and nothing could be done to check it. Attempts to stay ship failed, and with each failure the gap between boat and ship increased. It seemed impossible that a rowing boat could be expected to gain on the headlong leeward rush of the ship. What an appalling thought; five men adrift, with neither food nor water, fifteen hundred miles from the nearest land that they could under the most advantageous conditions hope to reach!

However, our hearts leapt with joy as we saw a tiny sail bobbing up and down between the long ocean rollers. We had no idea that the boat had a mast and sail in it. Letting all the sheets of our square sails fly, we at least reduced our speed; and, after a protracted struggle, five exhausted men in a boat filled with water to their knees eventually reached the ship side. So ended an abortive adventure.

When we came to the Equator we saw neither

a sail nor a puff of smoke. This was remarkable, because we were sailing across the track of all types of vessels, both outward and homeward bound. We had crossed the Equator alone twice in the same voyage. Most unusual!

A few days later, when off the mouth of the Amazon, we met an old friend of Rio days. Late in the afternoon, we saw on our port quarter a cloud of snow-white canvas. She was steering a little different course from ours and sailing at a great speed. We were able to compare positions with flag signals before darkness came. She turned out to be one of the Rio-Baltimore coffee clippers. Cutting our wake so close that we thought she had carried away our log line, she brushed by us like a real clipper! Four tall masts, smothered with perfect-fitting sails, her lee bow tinged with the red glow of her port light, gave her a Mephistophelean appearance as she stealthily stalked us in the darkness. A good thing it was night. There was no need to hide our faces in our hands, but we always fared badly in the tropics, and there was no actual need for it. It was a stupid idea that we must wear out old and ill-fitting canvas in the fine weather.

4

ALMOST A TRAGEDY

When we were about three hundred miles from Barbados an extraordinary thing happened, and it is difficult to reconcile the incident with the usual alertness that one is accustomed to expect from experienced sailors. The only excuse that can be put forward was the sublime weather and our proximity to the windward islands of the West Indies.

It was one of those days when the trade wind was in a brisk mood and we were scooting along like an express through a sea filled with white horses and the air equally full of flying fish. Never had we seen so many flying fish before. They must have been the season's exodus from their native Sargasso, meeting with stout opposition on their way to the various parts of the ocean. About two miles to our starboard was a white fishing boat sailing in our direction; and if they were out for flying fish, their luck was in. They could not have chosen a better spot. We were very shortly out of their sight. The Captain, who had been having his p.m. sleep, had not been told about the trivial incident, but during the course of casual conversation later in the day it came out that we had seen this fishing boat. He thought for an instant, then said angrily: "There can be no fishing boats out here. What right had any one to assume that it was a fishing boat? You must have passed a shipwrecked crew making for the islands." He was disposed to turn back and tack, hoping that we might pick the boat up again, but as the chances through approaching darkness were remote, we went on. It turned out that it was a shipwrecked crew. They were picked up the next day by a local trading schooner, and taken to one of the islands. We heard that their vessel had caught fire on the high seas, and that they had been many days in this open boat.

5

BRITISH TO THE BACKBONE

We anchored in Carlisle Bay, Bridgetown, Barbados, nineteen days after leaving Ascension. There is one thing about Barbados that stands out conspicuously—the people are British to the backbone. They are boastfully proud of being members of the Empire. The negroes look upon all Britishers who visit their island as real friends. There is a complete lack of shyness, and they make one feel that they have been counting the days for one's arrival in order to get news. Sincere and kind inquiries about the Queen and the Royal Family are fired at you by all and sundry. "And when did you last see them?" They demand details of the occasions: "And how does old England look?" and "Are we as happy as they are?" They have every reason to be proud of their allegiance, for the little island (about the size of the Isle of Wight), ever since it was first populated in the early part of the seventeenth century, has never been under any other rule but British. Most of the other islands have been French, Spanish, British, Dutch, or Portuguese in turn.

6

900,000 COCO-NUTS ARE UNSINKABLE

Discussions were rife on board as to our next loading port. One thing the Captain was fairly sure of was that it would be none of the phosphate ports, as he had delivered a mild ultimatum to the Owner that he considered the *Pride of Wales* no longer equal to the task. There was a large and selective number of ports to our leeward. Would it be log wood from Central America or timber from the Southern States, molasses, rum, sugar, cotton, or coffee from the many fertile islands? But no one had guessed that it would be Trinidad to load coco-nuts for London.

When the Captain learned this good news he flushed with shame, for although the Owner had considered his wishes, he could see behind the decision a touch of silent sarcasm. He had gone to the other extreme, for however vile the weather, we were now unsinkable; however long the passage, we could not starve. Moreover, the coco-nuts were so light that we would be high enough out of the water, and the ship so buoyant that we would be out of reach of the highest sea, which was another great advantage.

When we examined our actual orders, they seemed almost a joke. We were to proceed to Mayaro Bay, situated on the eastern side of Trinidad, the weather side of the island. Here, without approaching nearer than two miles of the beach, we were to look for a tall flagstaff erected on the shore. There were many of these flagstaffs along the eight-mile stretch of the bay, but ours had to be a certain scheme of colours, red, white and blue, or any other combination of colours that the Shippers chose to select. We found our flagstaff somewhere near the middle of the bay, and here we had to anchor, virtually in the middle of the ocean, unprotected from wind or sea, with the beach where the long Atlantic rollers pounded themselves to pieces under our lee. We were the only fool in the place. We were warned at Barbados that we should require both anchors, each out at full cable. If our orders seemed a joke, our first attempt at carrying them out was beyond it. Here was a sailing vessel with only forty tons of ballast on board riding bows under, off a lee shore. The only consoling feature was that we put implicit trust in the good weather which more or less all the year round frequented these parts, and we hoped that the first day was an exception. It was blowing fairly hard, and the sea was such that it gushed through the hose pipes at each plunge and threw spray over the cat heads. We were now very pleased that we had overhauled our cable, for it was going through the acid test with a vengeance. The old ship was tugging at it in real earnest. We flew our recognition numbers all that day, but no one responded. We could see people walking along a road between the beach and the fringe of the dense forest of coco-nut trees, but they just passed by. It was easy to understand that communication between shore and ship was out of the question as the huge breakers, which could be seen from aloft with binoculars, crashed up the beach for a distance of half a mile.

On the afternoon of the second day we launched the lifeboat, with the idea of making a reconnaissance of the place. Six of our heaviest men and the Captain set off. To watch the event, I took up a good position in the main top with a telescope, and I was thus able to bring the beach almost to our stern. When the boat had reached a position about a mile from the shore, scores of negroes rushed down the beach and energetically waved the crew back. The advice was superfluous, as

the Captain had seen the position of things and
had his boat facing the sea and wind. When they
returned they reported that the landing conditions
were impossible, and the Captain could not for
the life of him see how they could load us from
such a place. But on the third day we noticed a
great deal of activity on the beach. From the
midst of a tumult of negroes, we could see a lighter
being tossed high by the surf and making slowly
for sea. Forced against the wind and sea by many
oars, she steadily approached. She had brought
us our first consignment of coco-nuts. For fourteen
days the procession went on until the count of
nine hundred thousand was reached, which was
our fill.

The freight was paid on the number of nuts
carried, so that every nut was counted on board.
Each lighter brought about twenty men. Ten
remained on the lighter, and the others filed along
the deck and down the hold, and along the line
the coco-nuts ran. A buck negro took up his
position in the main rigging. He was the tallyman,
and by his side was a basket containing a few
small green coco-nuts with their tails attached.
The ten men in the lighter each threw on deck
two nuts so that five shies was tally, meaning a
hundred nuts. It was necessary that they all threw
at the same time. A delinquent was reminded by
the tallyman who hurled at him one of the hard
green variety, which if it landed on him would
persuade him that he must not be late again.
If two or three failed to keep time, a regular
bombardment took place and they fled in all
directions. He would yell: "No. 4, black trash, I
kill you."

I went ashore many times in an empty lighter and returned later in a full one. It gave time to look round and see the forest and have a chat with one and another. A track of lovely sand stretches for miles, perpetually washed by surf of imposing magnitude and beauty of colour. It was no uncommon sight to see a breaker tearing up the beach for a distance of half a mile. From this embroidery of snow-white sea merged soft-toning shades of green extending seaward a mile, to be lost in the azure blue of the Atlantic. Due to this part of the island's close geographical relationship to the vast northern coast line of the South American continent, it became the recipient of a weird assortment and an abnormal quantity of flotsam and jetsam. Lumber and timber carried away by the two great rivers Amazon and Orinoco, on reaching the sea, were turned by wind and current influences in the direction of Trinidad. Negroes patrolled the beach daily at an early hour, and made useful collections. Their huts and out-buildings and furniture were mostly built and kept in repair by the timber picked up on the beach. Portuguese men-o'-war, too, for the same reason, were blown into the bay in huge shoals. The expanse of foreshore, already speckled with richly-tinted sea shells, was further embellished with myriads of tiny rainbows. These were stranded Portuguese men-o'-war that had been hurled high and dry by the great breakers. These quaint-looking sea creatures look most attractive as they float by on the waves in thick shoals, reminiscent of a fleet manœuvring in the breeze. They are of the jelly-fish variety. The portion above the surface resembles a small and slightly-elongated

balloon, and when the light plays on this frail
structure it reflects delightful iridescent shades.
They can deflate and sink at will, and rise again.
But there ends their charm. Woe betide the human
skin that deigns to chafe their beauty, for they
are a living mass of virulent and irritant poison.
I could but think, as I rested a while mid the
constant roar of the sea and the gentle whistle
of the bland breeze, leaning against a background
of miles of tall coco-nut trees which fanned a
cloudless sky, how grand and majestic it all was.
Did it make up for the hard life in a small three-
hundred-ton sailing vessel? Yes, it did; it was
all worth while—and wonderful.

I was invited during one of my visits ashore
to look up one of the tallymen who had a cabin
on the edge of the plantation, and I must say
they gave me a right royal welcome. It was amazing
how such a large family packed away so neatly
into such a small place; but the truth is, they
only wanted somewhere to sleep. Their lives are
lived in the open, and they are all occupied on
the plantation. He had a large and voluminous
wife, who worked harder than all the other members
of the family put together, it seemed, and with
it all she was most good-natured and cheerful.
The place was surrounded by little black children
with fat tummies. She was proud to say they
were all hers, and when I told her that my brothers
and sisters had numbered more than a dozen, she
looked reproachfully at her husband—they only
had ten up to date! For my special benefit the
tallyman organised a race between two of his boys
—the track was up a coco palm. I was surprised
to see with what dexterity and ease these boys

ran up about thirty feet of barren and perpendicular trunks. They climbed much like monkeys, the feet being always flat on the tree. But the more sober-minded plantation worker when collecting the nuts achieves the same end by using a sling or a strop round the tree and round his body against which he reclines as he climbs, particularly when he gets to the top where the fruit is and it is necessary to use both hands for his work. The coco-nut enters largely into every phase of their lives, so much so that it is difficult to imagine how it is possible for human beings to dispense with its use. The green nut contains its fill of a delicious and cool sweet milk—even in the hottest weather, and exposed to the sun it still remains cool, due to the husk being a bad conductor of heat. The actual nutty part, as we know it in England, is in the fruit's early stages a rich cream, which is eaten with a spoon, and is sustaining. As the fruit ripens so it becomes hard. It is then very rich in oily products, which are, when extracted, used for lighting and heating and cooking. The fibre of the husk is used for brushes, mats, ropes, etc., and the shell is most handy as a domestic vessel.

I had brought articles of clothing ashore which the tallyman said his "Dinah" would mend and launder for me. I do not think I have ever seen clothes dry so quickly as they did here. That constant and fresh sun-saturated breeze had wonderful drying and bleaching properties. While I sat on a log outside the hut, yarning and smoking and showing the youngsters sailor's knots, in which they were deeply interested, the work was busily going on to the cheerful hum of a plantation tune.

Parrots, too, screeched pleasantly in the branches above. Mounted on mules, we galloped down endless avenues and green glades of coco trees, spaced out with the regularity of soldiers on parade. Directly under the trees was a brown carpet formed of decayed leaves and branches, and here and there could be seen large nuts that had fallen off the trees, looking much like human heads, for when dry the husk cracks and exposes the inside fibre, which from the distance looks much like human hair. There were conflicting stories as to the origin of this great and wonderful belt of palms, but it is feasible to give credulence to a romantic explanation that a ship carrying a cargo of coco-nuts— which were brought to this side of the world from the other with the idea of attempting to cultivate the species in the West Indies—was wrecked in a storm and her cargo washed ashore all along the eastern side of the island, much as the logs and the Portuguese men-o'-war were. The regularity of the rows could be accounted for by the variable high-water mark, governed by the changeable velocity of the wind.

Less than half a mile landwards from the beach were lagoons and mangrove swamps. The surrounding country, closely knitted with undergrowth and dense forests, teemed with reptiles, weird birds, and beasts of prey. Boa-constrictors were there in plenty; alligators, too, could be heard bellowing in the distance. The variety of insects, both with venomous and innocent habits, were there in staggering proportions, but they did keep within bounds, and rarely disturbed the peace of the colony. Mosquitoes kept away, probably because of their inability to battle against the prevalent wind.

On board ship we were not so fortunate. Our queer cargo brought many disagreeable strangers to disturb our peace and to inject virulence into our veins. Sailors had to endure, with much fortitude, interference and discomfort from the commoner variety of rodents, vermin, and insects permanently sharing their lives with them; but now were added to our already strong contingent of objectionable life—scorpions, centipedes, millipedes, and innumerable other insects of unknown source to us. They came on board as stowaways, hidden in the corners and crevices of the hospitable husks of the nuts. They were small when they came, but soon grew to normal proportions. They would at set of sun emerge from their seclusion in a desperate search for food. Some would crawl, others creep, and some would leap into our living quarters, leaving no locker or bunk unexplored. Most unnerving. Scorpion stings were of common occurrence, but no one succumbed. The negroes had warned us and given us first-aid information. Our *nouveaux arriveés* were apparently made none too welcome. The old residents of the ship objected to their presence. Terrified to sleep, I could hear close by in the linings, near my bunk, much commotion and the squealing of excitable rats, which went on interminably. Either our tropical visitors were overpowered and exterminated or they did not like ship life, for they quickly disappeared. They say that the scorpion, when facing death from prairie fire, could commit suicide by stinging himself. Perhaps he thought life in a wind-jammer equally awful, and called for the same extreme measure.

7

SEA SHANTIES AND A GRAND SAILING DAY

The negroes of Trinidad are the African type.
They are particularly musical, and during spare
time they used to entertain us with their fine voices,
singing their own inimitable spirituals with wonderful harmony and effect. They made the Captain
promise that on our sailing day they would be
allowed to help us weigh anchor and set sail.
They were soon conversant with our sea shanties
and sang them lustily on every possible occasion.
Our sailing day was going to be a gala day for them.
They were quite at home in a ship and knew all
the sails and ropes by name, but their extreme skill
was in evidence when manœuvring a lighter through
the surf. The day we finished loading the two lighters remained alongside until tea-time, when the
crews of both were entertained to tea, which com-
prised ship's biscuits and black tea. Had we
lavished a feast on them they could not have shown
more gratitude or, I feel sure, enjoyed it more.
They sat down on deck round the hatches, and
it was a pleasure to see them, with their beautiful
white teeth, showing us how ship's biscuits should
be devoured. After tea we saw some weird dancing
and heard some excellent singing. It is astonishing
the feeling and artistry they are able to command
when they express themselves in their spiritual
glees.

Our day of sailing was drawing near, but there
was no occasion for us to worry about weighing
anchor—which normally, with a hundred fathoms
out on each cable, would be tedious and hard work

of hours' duration—for we were to have a grand
send-off from our lightermen. This had been
almost sacredly promised. One early morning,
conditions were favourable to get under weigh.
Our ensign smacked the breeze as it signalled our
farewell to Mayaro Bay. A lifeboat hurrying to
succour a ship in distress would have been proud
of the despatch with which these rollicking gay-
hearted negroes splashed through the surf to wish
us adieu, their clumsy craft leaping from wave to
wave, throwing high the spray to a swinging
melody and the strains of many accordions. Their
excitement was such that they clambered over the
ship's side like a lot of schoolboys.

Special gadgets had been attached to the windlass so that every one could play his part and do
his share. The accordion players took up their
positions on the fore-hatch. I had heard shanties
ringing through the air at Falmouth from the
fo'c'sle head of famous ships and also at Rio, but
they withered into insignificance when compared
with this festival of harmony. I shall ever enjoy
and cherish happy memories of that sailing day.
It really was grand.

To the great delight of our passengers, we did
a short leg to the southward with their lighter
towing astern. We soon had all sails set, and as
our best canvas was bent in anticipation of stormy
weather ahead, we were cleaving swiftly and cleanly
through the sea. Heading now for the North
Atlantic, we cast adrift the lighter and its jolly
crew. Having responded to their hearty cheers
with a dip of the ensign, we started on the long
journey home.

8

SEEKING A WAY OUT

Our intention was to weather the string of islands and make for the open ocean via the Sargasso Sea, but things did not go quite to plan. Our greatest difficulty was to sail the ship; she was sitting so lightly on the sea that she resembled a hayrick more than a ship, and certainly behaved like one. She just went where the wind blew her, but we were not complaining; life was most pleasant. We managed to get out of Mayaro Bay, and by the close of the day we were hugging the lee of Tobago. The setting sun was bathing one of the prettiest of the islands with a crimson glow.

Tobago is known to every school boy and girl throughout the world as the legendary island which Defoe used for *Robinson Crusoe*.[1] For scenic effect, charm of setting and realism of atmosphere, his choice could not be improved upon. Those delightful strands, adorned on the one side by the artistic cabbage palm and on the other by a wilderness of tropical vegetation surmounted by rugged and rocky eminences, were the very back-ground for the most popular adventure in fiction.

On sighting St. Lucia we were convinced that our scheme of fetching the open ocean would have to be abandoned, and that we should have to break through between the islands into the Caribbean Sea, and endeavour to escape into the open

---

[1] The "Adventures of Robinson Crusoe," although founded on the experiences of one Alexander Selkirk in the island of Juan Fernandez, were undoubtedly written by Defoe with the island of Tobago in mind. He was possibly influenced in this direction by the graphic description of the island in the writings of Captain John Poyntz.

through the Sambrero Passage. I was very glad
of this, for we had five days of rapturous sailing,
brushing close to Martinique, Dominica, Guadaloupe, St. Kitts, Monserrat, and numerous other
small islands. As it was so convenient, we put in
at Port Castries, capital of St. Lucia, for stores
that we were unable to procure at Mayaro. This
was a very delightful harbour, land-locked and
surrounded by beautiful country, thickly wooded
with an endless variety of tropical scenery, whilst
high, irregular volcanic mountains, studded at
frequent intervals by forests of palms filled up the
background until they were lost in clouds. St.
Lucia appears prominent in English history. It
played an important part as a naval base during
the troublous days between England and France
in the eighteenth and nineteenth centuries.

Although we kept very good wind along Martinique, we passed quite close to St. Pierre (which
we had visited on the second voyage), and pleasing
puffs of rum were conveyed to us on the wings of
the wind. After that we were hard put to it to
fetch anywhere near Monserrat, the little green
island famous for its lime juice, which is such a
familiar beverage with all deep-sea mariners. But
our luck was out. The wind dropped for a whole
day, and we fell a victim to the weird and confused
currents which swept us to leeward at a great rate.
The verdict was that we had missed Sambrero
Passage, and were extricating ourselves with some
anxiety through a maze of volcanic islands and
stray rocks, known as the Virgin Islands, the
largest of which is Tortola, under British rule.
We literally grazed along the northern shores of
that delightful island, Santa Cruz. It was a miracle

R

we did not foul a perilous-looking headland. We were surrounded by breakers. We had missed Sambrero Passage! This meant trying our fortune through Mona Passage, two hundred and fifty miles to the westward, and we were now getting anxious, as Mona could not be looked upon as a certainty, and that would mean running down as far as Cuba for the windward passage. Since we had left Mayaro we had been steadily increasing our distance from England instead of decreasing it—not quite a profitable procedure. Before we had gone much further, we sailed right into a tornado.

This is the story of it. It was a lovely night, nearing four bells of the first watch. The large island of Porto Rico towered above us on our weather, and the small island of Mona, which is a sentinel in the middle of the fair-way, lay slightly under our lee. The port watch was on deck, and the weather had been so fine that we were lost in our own complacency and worried little about barometric pressure.

Bob and I were yarning on the fo'c'sle head; John, the big German, had the wheel, and the Chief paced the poop. The old ship was in excellent fettle, moving briskly through a calm enough sea, every sail filled with a breeze that was saturated with a refreshing dew. A more ideal night at sea and more favourable conditions for negotiating the narrow Mona Passage could not be wished; and yet within ten short minutes we lay forlorn and helpless. A tornado passed our way and left its malediction. Our neat little packet of a quarter of an hour since was suddenly whipped into a shambles. Eighteen of our best sails that we had

just put up at Mayaro had been rudely ripped
from their stays and blown far into the sea. Our
clean and trim decks resembled a bric-à-brac
store. Brand-new running gear, rove but a week,
were rent asunder like so many rope yarns. Tangled
braces hung in festoons through the deck-ports
and trailed the sea. Torn sails that had fouled
the rigging draped the shrouds with rags and
tatters.

When boasting that we were safe from stress
of weather while carrying this wonderful cargo,
we had overlooked the fact that ships can turn
turtle; and when this diabolical blast caught us
just abaft the weather-beam and sent us reeling
on our beam-ends, this ghastly possibility seemed
imminent. As Bob and I were thrown into the
lee-scuppers, we were in the right spot to fully
realise this danger. Two men of the watch below,
who were sleeping on the main-hatch, rolled there
to join us. Petrified with fear, my ears deafened
by the rushing of the sea—for we were tearing
along, the shrieking of the wind and the distressing
noise of sheetless sails flapping to shreds—I saw
the great mainsail torn from its yard and carried
away like a handkerchief. Our closeness to the
high-weather shore of Porto Rico, which blacked
out almost the entire horizon on that side, was
probably the cause of us being caught so unpre-
pared. Ordinarily, away from land, it would have
been impossible that such a disturbance, which
is always accompanied by unusual cloud formations, could have escaped our notice. Within
a few minutes, all was over, and the brave little
ship sat bolt upright and seemed to say: "I'm
all right, but where are my wings?" All that

remained were the brand-new No. 1 canvas, lower topsails (storm sails), and the storm jib. The barren spars, decorated here and there with dangling remnants of canvas, gave the ship a spectral appearance against the starlit sky.

The rest of the night was spent in digging old and odd sails from the sail-lockers and hurrying them into position. We had little to spare if we meant to negotiate Mona Straits. Those few minutes had not only cost us many pounds in money, but also robbed us of the confidence that only good sails can give in heavy weather. Although we were eight hundred miles from Trinidad, we were in reality four hundred miles further away from England than we should have been under ordinary circumstances and conditions, and we had been a week at sea.

But a sudden change came over the scene. Hardly had we finished bending to the spars old sails of some of which we were profoundly ashamed, than Father Neptune beckoned us to line up. He had entered us for a four-thousand mile time race. Crossing the starting line, which was close to the shores of that rugged and mountainous island of Santo Domingo, we were off to the crack of a smart breeze like a rocket; and this time we never looked back, which was most unusual. Little did we imagine, as we rolled lazily on a calm sea, sweltering under the torrid rays of the sun on this 13th day of December, 1891, that we should be towing up dear old Thames as the church bells of Greenwich and the sirens of steamers, bells of sailing ships, and the shrill whistles of railway engines, were fanfaring the old year out and the new in. The four thousand miles that our log registered were covered in eighteen days; and with better steering at least another day could have been knocked off. There were few steamers in those days that could have improved on this performance, and many that could not equal it. We made no fuss, although we thought it must have been a record for a ship of that size. We were lucky, because the wind never changed in direction and little in force the whole time, and owing to the coco-nuts the old ship was only drawing 9 ft. 6 in instead of the usual 14 ft. 6 in. It was not a case of sailing home, but being literally blown home.

9

A FIGHT IN A STORM

An exciting time was experienced passing through the Forties, where a succession of rousing gales drove us along like a balloon. There were three days when we registered over two hundred and thirty miles in the twenty-four hours, but steering was very difficult; it was the very devil. Four points each side of her course was the best that we could do, and at the end of two hours at the wheel one was exhausted. We never had more than six sails set at a time, and in the heavy squalls but four. The faster we went the more difficult was the steering.

One very stormy night, running hard before a terrific gale, under reef foresail, fore lower top-sail, reef main upper-top sail and main lower-top sail, we had an anxious time because we feared in the heavy yaws that the masts would go over the side. Bob had the last trick at the wheel in the first night watch, and poor old Bob was doing very badly—so badly that the Mate had perforce to stand close and watch him. This made matters worse. "Can't you steer the damned ship better than that?" "I am doing my best, sir." "Look out! Can't you see she is going? Check, man! Check her, man!" But Bob was too late, we were now nearly broadside on. This was more than the Mate could tolerate. He completely lost his temper, and struck Bob a heavy backhander in the mouth with his ringed hand, cutting his lip through and smashing a tooth. Instantly Bob jumped to battle, gale or no gale, leaving the wheel to spin at a terrific rate. I made for the wheel in an endeavour to secure it and save the situation, but it struck me a nasty blow in the arm, and I thought it was broken. All this time the fight was raging fiercely and had moved towards the break of the poop, a dangerous place, for it meant a five-foot drop for one or the other, or both. Welsh epithets and German curses rent the storm.

The spinning of the wheel had awakened the Captain, and he came to the top of the companion-way and helped me to get the ship back on her course. I told him what was happening, and that the fighters had both fallen on the main-deck, and were still fighting furiously. As the Mate had struck the first blow, the Captain thought it best not to interfere, so he went below again and waited for news, which I was supposed to carry to him.

Bob came back to the wheel with his hands and face smothered with blood and his mouth a terrific size, but he was good-looking compared with the Mate, who crawled along a little later, much the worse for wear, with both eyes partially closed and his angular features rounded off by swellings and abrasions; and he was limping badly also. He took up his position, much in the same place as before, and Bob's steering was just as bad. I shrivelled with each yaw, but at midnight the tension was raised, but only until four, when we came on deck again, a crippled and bedraggled party. Bob and I were soon put to work. "Shake the reef out of the main upper top sail," was the first staggering order, savouring all through with refreshing revenge. The wind may have dropped a little, but it was still a filthy night, and the ship was squirming through towering seas and chasing from one side of the ocean to the other. We hoped that the yard would have been lowered and brought to rest on its topping-lift. This would have made the job reasonably easy. But no! It had to be done the way that entailed the greater difficulty.

Bob, who was twice my size and as strong as a horse, and had been more years at sea, got on quite well with his yard-arm, and was soon back in the mast, leaving a trail of flapping sail; but things had gone badly with me. I almost fell into the sea. I even now get the cold shivers when I think of that awful experience. With heavy sea-boots on, which were smeared with dubbin, I slipped, but fortunately a leg went each side of the foot-rope, and by some miracle I was able to get hold of the topping-lift. Here I swayed and swung and yelled until my throat bled, but it was so dark that no one could see me. My shrieks reached no one's ear. The deafening roar of the sea and the piercing shrill of the wind whistling through the spars filled me with despair. Through sheer fright, I could feel my hold gradually breaking.

When Bob returned to the mast, he could see that something was wrong on my side, and hurrying to investigate found me swinging under the yard. His welcome and comforting vice-like grip lifted me safely back on the foot-rope. It is a horrible feeling to hang helplessly from the extremity of a flimsy spar, being flung and flailed at jerky random through a storm-swept space, wondering which would serve best my fate, either to be dashed to pieces against the angular deck fittings eighty feet below or be swallowed by cavernous billows.

The terrors of the infuriated elements are intensified tenfold during the grim hours of darkness. In many ships such an incident would not have been possible. Back ropes are fitted, against which a seaman can lean and derive a sense of comfort and security and also much assistance in the execution of his perilous duty, but in this ship it would be considered a superfluous expenditure of a length of rope. One was expected to work with both hands and possess the balance sense of a Blondin.

10

APPROACHING HOME

At daylight, the main top-gallant sail and fore upper-top sail were set, and it was evident that the Captain was in earnest mood to benefit to the utmost from any force of wind that came from a westerly direction. For the first time I saw preventer back-stays being rigged from the main top-gallant mast. This meant business, and it seemed to herald an exciting and thrilling time for the next twenty-four hours, which, however, nearly culminated in disaster. From noon to noon we passed the 230 mark, and during one heavy squall we logged twelve knots. The wind was N.N.W., so that all six sails were in action, and, with a quartering sea, steering was much better. All agreed that we were running before the heaviest sea ever that afternoon; one sea measured thirty-seven feet, and during a quarter of an hour spent by the Captain in the main-rigging, the average sea was thirty-two feet. He called me up to see a wonderful sight. Far away on the northern horizon we could see the hull of a large liner enveloped in a haze of spray. Her two black funnels were emitting dense clouds of bewildered smoke. Crashing into the teeth of the storm, she was plunging into the sea as far as the foremast. Cascades of ocean poured over her side as she lifted her bow in the air, but it was most exciting when she appeared to mistime a big one and buried her clipper bow into the side of a mountain, so to speak. She was one of the Atlantic record-breakers for Britain during that epoch. Two white rings on black funnels and three masts disclosed her identity to be either *City of New York* or *City of Paris*, hailing from Liverpool. Although she boasted of a tonnage displacement of eleven thousand against our three hundred, yet on that occasion we were definitely the faster ship, and the drier. It was our turn to crow. Speed before a sea and speed against a sea are entirely different propositions. We doubted very much if the liner was exceeding six knots. The sun peeped at us through the frowns of angry clouds and stayed long enough to enable us to work out our positions.

The next occasion to verify the same was six days later, when we ran into the welcome glow of the light of Eddystone lighthouse. The dead reckoning navigations of the mariners of those days was nothing short of wizardry.

II

A DERELICT THREATENS US

Booming along from the drear of a long night through yet another boisterous and dank dawn, "This is something like sailing," was the Captain's cheerful bulletin, as he, the Mate, and I were sipping coffee. We were wedged in our respective corners round the cabin table, inhaling a vicious atmosphere of stale smoke, caused by an ill-functioning paraffin lamp which had been burning all night. A hundred and twenty miles in twelve hours, and given a continuance of the conditions until noon it should be the old ship's best run ever." Then turning to me with a sparkle in his blue eyes, mingled with a doubtful pucker of the brow, he added: "Won't your grandfather be pleased with our performance! Do you think he will present me with a new hat as a token of his appreciation?"

His pleasantries were rudely interrupted by a panic shriek from one of the helmsmen: "A ship in distress right ahead. Come quickly, sir! We are closing on her fast!" As we scrambled on deck, we met the boatswain, who was in charge of the watch. He was returning from the fo'c'sle head, where he had been making closer observations. "It is a derelict, sir, and has changed

her course three times in as many minutes."
Something had to be done quickly, as we were
rushing headlong towards disaster.

What happened before our ship was manœuvred clear of this dangerous obstruction will ever
remain one of the most dramatic episodes of my
sea life. The derelict was a white-painted barque
of foreign appearance of about six hundred tons.
Two tattered storm square sails were still set,
but many other sails had partially blown adrift
and flapped in the gale. The heavy lower yards
were free and raced round the masts in keeping
with her capers. When her sails filled on a tack,
these yards rested taut on the back-stays. This
gave her an amazing spurt until, of course, she
fouled the wind again. The situation had suddenly
developed into a pitched battle between a ship
skilfully handled and game to obey any reasonable
command, versus the elements in their vilest and
wildest mood. It was an occasion when the weather
alone was quite sufficient to combat, but when the
wild rushes of this unchained terror were thrown
into the fray against us as well, our chances of
pulling through became obscure, to say the least.
She had compelled us to alter course twice already.
We had too much canvas on to carry out manœuvres
of this description. It looked at one period that
we might get clear, but the situation changed in
a flash, and things became critical. The derelict's
sails filled, and she gathered way. It looked for
all the world as if she were making a mad attempt
to cut off our escape. We were now being forced
to a broadside-on position. We were being driven
into a corner, so to speak. The wind shrieked
through the shrouds. Would our sails hold? Would

our masts stand? We tried to take the huge fore-sail in, but the ship's angle was so steep that she seemed to be falling on her beam ends, going over more and more every second. Great seas now swept over us, our position for'ard was becoming untenable; we had to leave the foresail to its fate.

We were becoming unmanageable through sheer speed, brought about by excessive sail pressure. The derelict was now close under our lee. She had suddenly fouled the wind and had given up the chase. Our hearts were cheered as we rounded her smartly to continue on our course. We were clear of one of the greatest dangers lurking in the sea. This battered and tangled mass gave the storm-swept space an eerie atmosphere. From her mizzen flew the remnant of the French tricolour, and the international signal of distress. Her cabin doors were open, and banged incessantly. The davit-falls crashed against her side with each roll. This told us that her lifeboat had been launched. It was most spectacular to see her broadside on. The great seas crashed over her, reaching fifty feet up her masts; and when struck she was thrown almost flat on the sea, but recovered in time to receive the next blow.

A week later, we learned that she had been found by a British warship and taken into custody, but she had travelled six hundred miles from that spot in the time.

Interested spectators to this thrill were the stormy petrel. They had forgathered in goodly numbers. They seemed to know there was drama afoot. They revelled mid the snarling and ferocious waves—visiting both ships in turn.

Darkie thought they were disappointed in the
performance. What at one time had looked like
a gala effort had fizzled out to a mere incident.
What a feast for them had we been grabbed
by this ocean ghost and dragged to eternity. It
could easily have happened had we arrived there
an hour earlier when it was dark.

12

"DARKIE" AND "YON"

"Darkie," whose name I have just mentioned,
was a copper-skinned seaman of the true Dago
type; but "Darkie" was a sick man and did not
look like lasting out many more moons. Short of
stature, his wizened face, deeply lined, bore traces
of the rigours of forty years at sea. Gold ear-rings
were suspended from the lobes of his long ears.
He was a brave little fellow, who rarely complained
about his health or his luck. He never failed to
turn out and do his job, whenever his watch came
round. But I should think, in his heyday, he was
a dangerous and rebellious little devil. I used to
endeavour to draw him out to tell me stories about
his life in deep-sea ships. He had much to say,
and his face bore many scars of tough encounters.
He would enthuse to a point, and then, finding
himself becoming involved as one of the ringleaders in some treacherous design destined to
disturb the peace of his ship, he would suddenly
recoil—"Ah, well, it's a hard life, and I wish you
luck, sir." He had been much interested by the
fight between the Chief and Bob—so much so
that his usual grim expression had been replaced

by a permanent ripple which his wrinkles accentuated, and gave him a sickly appearance. Had he been well enough, he could see in Bob and another chap called Yon wonderful material for staging a first-class mutiny. The fuse had been lighted. Yon was possessed of the finest physique of any human I had ever seen. He was a German. Tattooed from his knuckles to his waist, he looked a strange spectacle when stripped. In reality he was as docile as a child, but capable of prodigious efforts when roused. He could balance Morris on the palm of his right hand and me on his left and raise us both up to the full extension of his arms, over his head, and walk round the deck with us. He had been for years a "strong man" in a travelling circus. The Captain thought much of this kindly-disposed Goliath, and often used to chat to him about his experiences on village greens in circus kit. Moreover, he used to select him as his mate when doing some of his fancy jobs and hobbies. There was more in this than met the eye—for with the German at his side, the Captain could feel the balance of power in the event of a disturbance well in favour of the cabin. Although the hefty German claimed no pugilistic skill, he could put people across his knee and break them in two, if he chose. I am making this statement in no glib manner, for Morris had occasion to experience and remember his enormous strength. I will relate the incident.

Morris, who was still the right side of twenty, was a fine type of young fellow, but possessed that typical Celtic temperament which frequently embroiled him in unpleasant clashes with the more phlegmatic variety of our cosmopolitan crew. Like most sailors of that age, he found it difficult to observe that punctuality which is most essential on board ship. For instance, at the change of the watch. When the last bell of the eight had been struck, the watch that had been on duty expected to hear the welcome patter of feet hurrying to take over the arduous trick at the wheel, or the bleak and lonely look-out. It was my duty to call the watch on this occasion, and I gave Morris an extra shake, which in his muddled half-sleep he resented. Flourishing his arm blindly to slay me, he, instead, caught the corner of a sea chest, which badly lacerated his hand. On his way to relieve the German at the wheel, he met me in the darkness and struck me a blow in the face, which sent me reeling into the scuppers, cutting my head open on a ring-bolt in the deck as I fell. Yon found me in a bad mess on his way from the wheel, and promised to avenge what he considered to be an unreasonable action. This he did by pinning the struggling Morris across his knees and administering a typical nursery punishment with a rope's end. Morris had to stand for the rest of the way across the Atlantic. The Captain would rarely inquire the reason why So-and-So's face was out of shape. He believed in a general doctrine that a man usually got what he deserved; and up to a point the Captain's argument could be followed to a logical conclusion. For instance, Bob got his deserts, and so did the Mate. I got mine, and Morris got his. Moreover, individual disagreements, short of murder, were safety valves, for they kept the issue within narrow confines, which, from his view-point, was a healthy symptom.

13

AN UNPLEASANT CHRISTMAS

Christmas Eve was full of hustle and hard going. We ran into a nasty cross sea during the night, and conditions became as bad as they could be. Visibility, due to torrential rain, was at times negligible. Being in a two-way traffic latitude, we had an anxious time. We seemed to be travelling much too fast to be safe. It was odd to think that we had been continuously in storm centres for the last ten days, and kept in them as far as North Foreland with little variations from gale intensity, and with frequent bursts of hurricane force. This night, and all through Christmas Day, we got the latter in its true form. How the masts and sails stood was nothing short of a miracle. I used to be much intrigued by watching the foot of that wonderful sail, the foresail, quivering and tugging in an effort to lift the ship's bow out of the sea. One's attention was attracted more by this sail because at night it caught the rich glow of the green and red reflections of the navigation lights. It gave a touch of brightness to the drab surroundings. It was an awesome sight, too, looking aft from for'ard. When the ship was flat down in the trough, one wondered how she could ever recover in time before that onslaught, scowling thirty feet above, had crashed. These huge waves made me think of some maddened monster rushing after its prey. The Captain was loth to leave the deck this night. He strutted firmly with his swinging gait, stopping occasionally to regain his balance. He would fidget with his moustache. This meant anxiety. The foresail was reefed again, and the fore upper topsail taken in. He decided to leave the main top-gallant sail to its fate. It was an old sail, and would be sure to go if we touched it. I was awakened from my first sound slumber, only a few minutes after midnight, by much commotion and shouting. I jumped up nervously, wondering what could have happened, and dressed. In fact we were always on tenterhooks. "All hands on deck" rang out above the turmoil of the tempest. For the first time in ten days a great sea came over the stern and filled the after-quarters to a depth of two feet. It must have been a tremendous wave to poop a ship in such light trim. Two or three quick rolls, and our bunks and bedding were saturated. This was a pity, for it need not have happened. The last man up had left the companion-way open. Gaining the deck in a half-dazed manner, I spoke to Morris, who told me that there was a ship burning flares right ahead, which we concluded meant that she was in distress. "Clew up the main top-gallant sail;" "Lower away main upper topsail;" "Haul up foresail;" "Up the helm," etc., were orders rapidly executed; we were preparing to render assistance. We lost our faithful top-gallant sail; it went like tissue-paper. This brought the flares on our beam. We could now see the hull and the masts of a large four-masted sailing ship snugly hove-to under storm sails, dipping and lifting in the mountainous sea. We passed quite close under her stern. She was all right. They feared that we might not see her navigation lights. They knew by the position of ours that we were running before the gale at top speed. It was our duty to pass clear of her, so

s

she made sure of attracting our attention with the flares. It was a great sight, on such a stormy night. She was the harbinger of Christmas Day.

We spent a most unpleasant Christmas, little different from an ordinary day, but we enjoyed additional rations of tinned mutton. In addition, many more currants were flung into the plum duff as a special treat. I was allotted the task of experimenting in the manufacture of our national bonne-bouche—a species of toffee known as "cyflath." The result was a brittle mess, but edible.

14

A GLIMPSE OF THE CREW

A pleasant surprise was in store when dinner was over. It was announced that the main brace was to be spliced. This meant a tot of rum to all hands, a most welcome interlude in a rather depressing day. We forgathered at the break of the poop, and seasonable toasts were interchanged in a good and hearty way.

There is one thing about the rum that sailors drink—it does get there. It seems to race round the ribs and reach the finger-tips in no time. I shall ever remember that Christmas party of tough humanity, arranged in a semi-circle, rough-looking and weather-beaten, mouths watering in anticipation of that luscious nectar of the Indies. Each dirty and bearded face showed up in bold relief the bright and twinkling eyes which only sailors possess. What a typical subject they would have presented to a painter or a sculptor seeking the

ideal material and the true atmosphere to immor-
talise in his art a fast-disappearing type—four
Welshmen, two Germans, a Swede, a Dane, a
Mulatto, and a Negro. Yet among them were
two extremely good-looking fellows. One of them,
the Swedish boatswain, was strikingly handsome
as well. Although most unlike a Scandinavian in
colouring, he would have befitted the rôle of a
Roman gladiator to better effect. The other was
Morris, the Welsh boy. Morris, unlike the boatswain, was true to his race. Well set-up, of medium
stature, dark complexion, and perfect aquiline
features, large brown eyes with the usual white of
a delicate duck-egg blue—permanent laughing
wrinkles extended from the corners of his eyes,
heavy well-defined brows, each of which he could
raise separately in an intriguing manner when
engaged in an interesting conversation. The lower
part of his face, too, was well balanced and full
of expression, which always proved most alluring
to the fair sex. I have said little about the Dane.
He was one of those quiet and unassuming men
whom nobody would notice much, except possibly
a medical man, and he only with a desire to remove
his adenoids, which would perhaps help to close
his ever half-open mouth. This wrongly gave him
the appearance of being simpering. But he was
a good sailor, and an even better sail-maker. His
keen hobby was rat-catching, and he employed an
ingenious idea. A beef cask, greased inside, half-
filled with salt water, caught as many as fifty rats
in one night. The lid of the cask was delicately
balanced and counter-poised, so that when the
rodent stepped on it to devour a dainty piece of
pork it would be tipped into the water. The lid

would then automatically return to the original position, and so the process continued.

Up to noon another excellent day's run was recorded, only ten miles short of the record. If we had not met the four-master we probably would have topped it, although we appeared to be sailing almost as well and much more comfortably under the diminished canvas pressure. I looked in at the fo'c'sle door during the first dog watch and listened to three accordions which Johann, Darkie, and the Dane could manipulate with quite harmonious results. Darkie had had a good voice in his time (and had at an early age been connected with opera in some way), good enough to have earned for him the exalted appointment of Head Shantieman in almost every ship he had sailed in; and if true, this was saying something. Operatic arias were also among this little man's accomplishments, and I saw him on more than one occasion carried away by his love for music to a point of physical exhaustion in attempting to do justice to an old favourite. He found in Johann an enthusiastic supporter of good music. Johann would play classical waltzes of his country's famous composers for hours on end, and delighted the whole ship. During our short stay at Barbados, I can remember pleasure steamers, cruising the Bay on Sunday morning, crowd round our bows, entranced by the melodious strains flowing from his accordion, and he, emerging from his perch, which was the capstan on the fo'c'sle head, through avenues of drying shirts, would bow graciously his appreciation of their boisterous applause.

Meandering aft, despondent enough, I sat a

while on the steps of the poop to watch the light
of Christmas Day fade into the sea. As I listened
first to the distant music of the fo'c'sle and then
to the more realistic ring in the shrouds and the
furore of the gale, my thoughts strayed to my old
home. How far away it seemed, amidst those
Welsh hills! How distant, to my despairing heart!
Yet how near in my vivid imagination, which
conjured up picture after picture before my tortured mind! What bright lights I could see shining
from the windows, what blazing fires of logs in
the warm green-garlanded rooms, what succulent
odours wafted from the busy kitchen! Tears were
not perhaps far away from my eyes, as I thought
of that large and happy family revelling in the
spirit of joyous Yuletide, each one bedecked in
gay harlequinade, seated round a table! A little
misted it seemed to my remembrance by the seasoned and searching vapours of good things to
eat. Then the stately procession of the holly-
crowned pudding, the blue flame flickering and
dying around it. I could hear the very rustling
of the gay-coloured crackers, their miniature explosions mingling with the fun and merriment of
home and happy childhood.

15

A DELICATE OPERATION

On Boxing Day, conditions looked like being
more kindly disposed towards us. The sun tried
hard to break through, and we were most anxious
that it should in order to get a position worked
out. Alas, it flattered to deceive; but all round

there was a definite improvement in the weather, and we were in happy vein. We had broken into the last thousand miles. Although a thousand miles in a sailing ship can be a prodigious distance and take any time up to three weeks, on this occasion we ran through them in four and a half days. There was no holding us. The sail-makers, the Captain, and the Dane had been busy getting another top-gallant sail ready, and all hands were kept on deck to bend it. Doing my trick at the wheel between eight and ten in the morning, I had an exciting time watching this delicate and dangerous operation. The Dane and Johann were detailed to the yard-arms, while Bob and Morris were inside them, and Darkie at the bunt. The job was easy enough in fine weather, but full of anxiety on such a day. It was thrilling to watch the two yard-arm fellows when the ship rolled heavily through an arc of 60°, dangling from the clouds, it seemed, hanging on like grim death with one hand and wielding a marlinespike with the other. They were fine fellows.

When the old sail was eventually set, a titter ran round the ship, for it was anything but smart-looking; one leech was longer than the other, with the result that the yard was at an ugly cock-a-bill. The strips of new canvas added were much too taut, with the result that the rest of the sail was in a state of constant palpitation, which was most annoying, and noisy. Darkie, who considered himself a good sail-maker but had had nothing to do with this job, was extremely funny about it. He thought it should have the effect of closing the Dane's mouth for the rest of his life, and that it should take a lot of the spring out of the Captain's sprightly gait as well.

16

DEFYING SUPERSTITION

The appearance in the sky of a small strange
bird, which flew twice round the ship in an excited
but distressed manner, caused a deal of conster-
nation. It was a land bird; and as the nearest
land was some hundreds of miles away, the Azores,
our curiosity was intense. It eventually came to
rest on the main-top. What was it? From where
had it come? What was its mission? Darkie, that
King of Superstition, cast a gloom over the ship
by saying that he thought ill of the intrusion. No
land bird would fight through such tempestuous
skies except as bearer of an ill-omened message.
"The doom of the ship!" he exclaimed.

Bob and Morris decided to climb the rigging
to investigate its whereabouts, and we thought
this courageous of them, as Darkie had succeeded
in impressing all hands that any interference with
the stranger would bring death in its trail. They
went aloft together. We watched them in the
fading light negotiating the futtock-shrouds leading to the main-top. We could see them stooping.
They had found a homing pigeon, utterly exhausted,
huddled against the mast. Morris took it in his
hand, and placed it carefully inside his jersey,
before beginning the descent to the deck, where
we anxiously awaited them. Although beautifully
marked and possessing full plumage, its body was
emaciated. The Steward quickly prepared a tempt-
ing meal for it, consisting of crushed ship's biscuits
soaked in water, to which was added grains of
rice. But alas, it was apparent that its life was

fast ebbing. Its little head drooped, its eyes closed, and it died in Morris's hand. It carried no identification signs or marks that would have helped us to solve its mysterious appearance in so strange a place; but in view of the long-continued wild weather we concluded that it must have been a pet on some unlucky ship and had been set free to seek its own safety.

I have often wondered whether Darkie lived to know how near the truth his evil creed proved to be, or how accurately his superstitious prophecies foretold the fate of the ship and the two seamen concerned. Soon afterwards Morris perished with all companions in a ship called the *Eagle Eyed*. Her name was added to that long and tragic list of ships that never returned. Bob died at Santos, of yellow fever, during the *Pride of Wales's* next voyage, and the ship herself never completed that voyage. She was beaten to submission by a succession of heavy gales in January and February, and took the final plunge into the slimy ooze of the Atlantic quite close to the spot where the pigeon episode occurred. I could visualise her stately companions of days gone by, peacefully resting deep down, draped in sombre ribbons of flowing sea-weed, awaking to pay homage to yet another ship that was slipping through imponderable space to take her place amongst them. I could imagine them selecting an appropriate resting-place for her as she slowly approached, twisting and turning drowsily, her storm sails still set and her frail structure battered, testifying that in her last desperate fight, at the end of twenty-four years' service, she had died game.

17

MARGATE ROADS

Making the English Channel under wintry conditions, when the ship's position for the last twelve hundred miles had been determined by dead reckoning, is wrought with anxiety. Although the mouth of the Channel is wide—a hundred and thirty miles—it is none too wide when a wild zig-zag course has been steered over that long distance in from the ocean. Being a light ship, the Captain was more than anxious to keep as far away as he possibly could from both the French and the English coasts. He was mortally afraid of being caught on a lee shore. When darkness came we were surprised to see the light of Eddystone well abaft our port beam. This was our first indication of England, but we had been happy in our minds all that day, as we had been coming up against a more or less constant stream of traffic. They were mostly steamers far away on the northern horizon and out of range of flag signals.

The first actual land we sighted was off Beachy Head the next afternoon, when the famous Seven Sisters, attired in white, peeped at us through a gloomy sky with their usual cold dignity. Anyhow, we were very glad to see them. We hugged close the coast of Thanet and anchored far out in Margate Roads in the darkness and under wretched conditions, twenty-six days after leaving Trinidad. Towing up the Thames behind a smelly tug, we felt as proud as peacocks. It was rarely our privilege to tow a distance like this. It was the only

sane and safe thing to do, for we were a positive
danger to shipping and ourselves except under the
most favourable wind conditions. A little excitement was introduced into the tedium of towing
when midnight came, and we joined in with the
merry throng each side of the river to welcome
the New Year in. We brought our two bells and
fog horns into action and the old tug wasted a
good deal of useful steam blowing his siren. It
was all so splendidly gay. We finished 1891 in
grand style.

18

GOOD-BYE TO THE RED ROSE

We were the centre of attraction on the morrow
as we lay to the buoys in the middle of Regent's
Canal Dock, awaiting a berth. It had gone round
that we had crossed the Atlantic from the coast
of Porto Rico to North Foreland in eighteen days,
a straight line of about three thousand eight hundred miles, but we had made it over four thousand
miles by our atrocious steering. One ship evidently
knew us, for she flew the signal "Well done!"
She was a small barque called the *Edith Mary*,
and was under a permanent charter to carry
Government stores to Ascension. She had left the
island just a week prior to our arrival there. They
knew that we were being expected, and naturally
were much interested in our appearance in the
same dock which they had reached only twenty-
four hours earlier.

It is interesting to compare the times of the
two ships from Trinidad. The *Edith Mary* enjoyed
wonderfully fine weather with light winds almost

all the way; and not until she had reached the chops of the Channel did she run into bad weather. She was thirty days longer in crossing the Atlantic than our time, and that in spite of weathering the Antilles and fetching well out into the Ocean. But she lost many days in the seaweed of the Sargasso, and was getting a bit worried because provisions were running short. From there they basked in glorious sunshine and moved slowly until converging on our course four hundred miles from home.

The end of the *Edith Mary* was tragic. She left Ascension in September of 1904, bound for St. Johns, Newfoundland, but nothing was heard of her nor of her crew after that day.

.   .   .   .   .

Hailing the ship from the dockside and waiting for a boat to take me aboard, I got into conversation with some dock labourers. They said it was many a day since they had seen such a pretty ship in that dock; and as I looked at her, with her sails unfurled, drying in the breeze, bleached by the tropical sun, and washed white by the torrential rains of the Atlantic, her once rich dark-green sides now changed to a whitish blue, tarnished by the brine of the sea, her white deck fittings and holy-stoned decks meticulously clean, I must say she captured my imagination, too.

Walking along the dockside *en route* to the station to entrain for North Wales, I met the men coming back from the shipping office where they had been paid off. They were in a hilarious mood, and frequently tacked perilously near the edge of the dock. They had all visited the barber and looked strange without their facial trimmings. Darkie was not with them. He had been collected and taken to hospital, where he must have ended a long and adventurous career. I had great difficulty in getting clear, as handshakes and farewell greetings were exchanged many times over and with ever-increasing vigour and fervour.

Looking back at them clambering over the ship's side, my eyes fell for what was to be the last time on my ocean home. That dainty figure-head, too, caught my eye. It seemed to offer me the red rose and to have a special smile for me that day. When far away from home I frequently used to go out on the bowsprit shrouds to look at it. When things were awry, and luck was out, its kindly expression took me back to happier days. It cheered me.

I had been gazing at the effigy of my mother, to whose fond memory this book is dedicated.

19

THE UNFINISHED VOYAGE

Before the *Pride of Wales* sailed on what was a voyage of disaster ending in tragedy, the Captain wrote me the following letter:

My dear Harry,

I have been given to understand from the Owner that you have decided not to come with me this voyage. The fact that we are going to Santos is given as the reason. Well, I cannot blame you, nor those who have probably influenced you in this respect. Santos is a most unpleasant place, and as you know I have cause to remember and despise it—my pitted face will for all time bear witness of its horrors. On the eve of sailing I thought I would like to write to wish you good luck and to tell you how much I shall miss your cheerful companionship. The old cabin where we have been together so long cannot quite be the same. Somehow I am not looking forward to this trip. I am beginning to feel the strain that these long ocean voyages in small ships entail, and the *Pride of Wales* is getting no younger, as you know. . . .

Do write me from time to time and post me up in news of yourself and your movements.

My greetings to your people,

Yours very sincerely,

J. J. GRIFFITH.

P.S. Bob is coming with us again, and of course Nancy Wellington.

The *Pride of Wales* left London in February, 1892, bound for Santos, in S. America, with a general cargo. She was shadowed and stalked by misfortune, sickness, and death until she was abandoned in a sinking condition in mid Atlantic a year later. I am able to give an abridged account of the voyage from extracts of letters written by Captain Griffith.

Arriving at Santos in April they found the port in a state of complete disorder. The ravages of yellow fever and smallpox had brought shipping to a standstill. Dozens of ships lay at their anchors rotting in the scorching sun without a soul on board. The *Pride of Wales* joined them in this shipping cemetery and remained marooned for four months. Most of her crew died, including Bob. The Captain states that he attended the funerals of fifteen Captains of English ships.

The *Pride of Wales* eventually cleared the port with a mixed crew of indifferent quality, and headed for the small port of Cayo, in the state of

Mexico. Here she loaded for England, leaving about Christmas. All went well until they were abreast of Bermuda. Here she ran into the track of great storms. Disaster came early. Two of her crew were washed overboard and drowned. This was quickly followed by another calamity, her bowsprit and jib-boom were torn asunder by the rage of the storm; her foremast too was blown over the side. Surely the end was not far off? The inrush of the sea through her torn bow was slowly beating the frantic efforts of her exhausted crew. She was gradually sinking.

The final narrative of the *Pride of Wales* is connected with the homeward journey of a Norwegian barque, an old timber drogher.

She was limping disconsolately across the North Atlantic, weary and worn. She had had a gruelling time. The great storms had reduced her, too, to an unseaworthy condition. From dawn to dusk her dejected crew scanned the horizon hoping to catch a glimpse of a ship that would rescue them from further torture. Two sailors working aloft came breathlessly down to say they had sighted a sail far away to the eastward.

The weather that day was in a contrite mood. A disabled ship looked out of place on such a fine and sunny day. The good news of a sail in sight flashed quickly round their ship. Tired and sleepy men were soon on deck and there was much joy in their hearts.

Eager for news, these hardy Norsemen clustered round the Captain, who, with anxious expression, was training his telescope on the distant stranger. Slowly and with a voice filled with emotion he told them it was a barque partially dismasted.

Her sails were blown to shreds, her head was drooping in the sea, and she looked in a pitiable plight. Two flags flew from her rigging, and by their shape their meaning was obvious and unmistakable, "In distress." Presently the British ensign broke against the blue sky and four more flags were shown which told them the ship's name was *Pride of Wales.*

The kindly-hearted Norwegians threw despair to the wind. They were now hastening to succour a stricken comrade. The men who a short while ago were filled with anxiety had suddenly changed. Despondency had turned to cheerfulness and hope.

They could discern a small group of humans huddled on the after-part of the ship. They were Captain Griffith and six of his companions. Although tired and hungry, their limbs stiffened from exposure, they could not hide their joy. With outstretched arms they waved welcome as this Samaritan of the sea hobbled to their aid.

Rescue work was difficult. It always seems to be on the high sea. In this instance the *Pride of Wales* was awkward, and being completely out of control she meandered in a dazed sort of way all over the sea, with the result that the Norwegian had to keep her distance. Moreover, being down by the head, the *Pride of Wales* played peculiar pranks and threatened on occasion to slip from under their feet. The addition of extra men to the Norwegian's complement was a problem which had to be solved. This meant many journeys to and fro until the requisite amount of stores had been transferred. Fresh water, too, had to be carried from one ship to the other. This proved a long and tedious operation, but it was imperative as the rescuers themselves were on short rations. By the close of day most of the good work had been done. When darkness spread its pall over the sea, the two little ships parted company.

As Captain Griffith took a last glimpse at the *Pride of Wales* a lump came to his throat. For him it was a touching scene. With her head sinking lower and lower in the sea, she appeared to be kneeling in prayer. The end had come to a long and successful career of a plucky ship. She was left to perish, alone, in a great sea.